Home Office
Department of Health
Department of Education and Science
Welsh Office

Working Together

Under the Children Act 1989

A guide to arrangements for inter-agency co-operation for the protection of children from abuse

LONDON : HMSO

ISBN 0 11 321472 3

Preface

It is well established that good child protection work requires good inter-agency co-operation. It is important for all professionals to combine an open-minded attitude to alleged concerns about a child with decisive action when this is clearly indicated. Intervention in a family, particularly if court action is necessary, will have major implications for them even if the assessment eventually leads to a decision that no further action is required. Public confidence in the child protection system can only be maintained if a proper balance is struck avoiding unnecessary intrusion in families while protecting children at risk of significant harm.

This document, prepared jointly by the Department of Health, the Home Office, the Department of Education and Science and the Welsh Office, consolidates previous guidance on procedures for the protection of children and recommends developments aimed at making these more effective. It takes into account the requirements of the Children Act 1989 and lessons learned from individual cases which have caused public concern, as well as examples of good practice provided by a number of agencies. It does not attempt to provide guidelines on the practice of individual professions in the recognition of child abuse or subsequent care or treatment but is concerned with inter-professional and inter-agency co-operation. It should therefore be read in the light of relevant guidance issued to individual agencies and professions.

This guidance is issued under Section 7 of the Local Authority Social Services Act 1970, which requires local authorities in their social services functions to act under the general guidance of the Secretary of State. As such, this document does not have the full force of statute, but should be complied with unless local circumstances indicate exceptional reasons which justify a variation.

Contents

5	WORKING TOGETHER – INDIVIDUAL CASES	25

PART 1

INTRODUCTION

1.1 The Children Act 1989 provides a new framework for the care and protection of children. It establishes a new range of court orders to protect children with new criteria. The child's welfare is the court's paramount consideration. A general principle is laid down that delay is likely to prejudice the welfare of the child. The court has new powers to concern itself with the assessment of the child at the interim or emergency stage and with the child's contact with parents and others. Parents are given full opportunity to be involved in the process. The guardian ad litem has new duties in the interests of the child.

1.2 The Act introduces the concept of parental responsibility which is retained if the child is looked after by a local authority, even if the child becomes the subject of a court order. An emergency protection order or a care order will give parental responsibility to a local authority and it may also be given to a third party such as a relative by a residence order. This (and other orders under Section 8) is part of the range of orders available to the court.

1.3 The new approach to court work under the Act must influence and permeate the work of all professionals in all agencies involved in child protection. When a case goes to court it will be heard in the Family Proceedings Court by magistrates specially selected and trained in family and child matters. Some cases will be transferred to the County Court or the High Court. The court procedure will be the same, but the case will be heard by a judge rather than magistrates. The court can make a different order from the one requested. When reaching its decision, the court must be sure that making the order will be better for the child, and if the court cannot be convinced of this, it must make no order at all.

NEED TO WORK IN PARTNERSHIP WITH FAMILIES

1.4 Local authorities have, under the Children Act 1989, a general duty to safeguard and promote the welfare of children within their area who are in need and so far as is consistent with that duty to promote the upbringing of such children by their families. As parental responsibility for children is retained notwithstanding any court orders short of adoption, local authorities must work in partnership with parents, seeking court orders when compulsory action is indicated in the interests of the child but only when this is better for the child than working with the parents under voluntary arrangements.

1.5 Section 1(3) of the Children Act 1989 sets out the issues to which courts will have to have regard in particular when making or varying private law orders which are opposed and all public law orders under Part IV of the Act. These are the ascertainable wishes and feelings of the child concerned (considered in the light of the child's age and understanding); the child's physical, emotional and educational needs; the likely effect on the child of any change in his/her circumstances; the child's age, sex, background and any characteristics of his which the court considers relevant, any harm which he has suffered or is at risk of suffering, how capable the parents are of meeting his needs and the range of powers available to the court. Although not all cases will be the subject of court action, all staff working in the area of child protection should be aware of these and should use them to underpin their work which should always be sensitive to the culture and background of the child and family.

1.6 Under Section 22 the local authority looking after a child or proposing to do so must give consideration, having regard to the age and understanding of the child, to his or her wishes and feelings, religious persuasion, racial origin and cultural and linguistic background. This is in addition to the wishes and feelings of the parents and others with parental responsibility.

1.7 *It is against this background* that agencies should operate the child protection provisions of the Act, which are designed to promote decisive action when necessary to protect children from abuse or neglect, combined with reasonable opportunities for parents, the children themselves and others to present their points of view.

1.8 Agencies should ensure that staff who are concerned with the protection of children from abuse understand that this assumption in the Act of a high degree of co-operation between parents and local authorities requires a concerted approach to inter-disciplinary and inter-agency working.

AREA CHILD PROTECTION COMMITTEES

1.9 The protection of children requires a close working relationship between social services departments, the police service, medical practitioners, community health workers, schools, voluntary agencies and others. Co-operation at the individual case level needs to be supported by joint agency and management policies for child protection. There must be a recognised joint forum for developing, monitoring and reviewing child protection policies. This forum is the Area Child Protection Committee (ACPC). Its role, functions and lines of accountability are described in Part 2 of this Guide.

LEGAL FRAMEWORK

1.10 Everyone who is concerned in a professional capacity with the protection of children needs to have a clear understanding of the main points of child care law as it applies to the care and protection of children, and its implications for the discharge of their respective responsibilities. They should be aware, in particular, that legislation places the primary responsibility for the care and protection of abused children and children at risk of abuse on local authorities; and that the nature of the responsibility carried by a local authority in an individual case will vary according to whether or not there has been court intervention and on the outcome of any proceedings. All practitioners need to be familiar with the main outline of the court procedure and in particular with the criteria for emergency protection orders, child assessment orders, care and supervision orders, and what effect these orders have if granted. This does not lessen the duty of everyone who is involved in child protection matters to work within national guidelines and local procedures agreed by the Area Child Protection Committee.

1.11 Other agencies besides local authorities have statutory duties or powers and all agencies have specific functions and professional objectives. In working together for the protection of children, however, they need to understand that they are not only carrying out their own agency's functions but are also making, individually and collectively, a vital contribution to advising and assisting the local authority in the discharge of its child protection and child care duties. **Therefore it is essential that Area Child Protection Committee procedures provide a mechanism whereby, wherever one agency becomes concerned that a child may be at risk, it shares its information with other agencies.** Other agencies may have information which could clarify the situation; there should be frequent sharing of concerns. If there is a need for *formal* procedures these should be implemented at the earliest possible stage and in respect of every allegation. Such procedures apply whether the child is living at home, with foster carers, in a residential home or school or in any other situation.

1.12 Agencies should ensure that their staff have access to the local ACPC handbook and know how to use their agency's child protection procedure.

1.13 The difficulties of assessing the risk of harm to a child should not be underestimated. It is imperative that everyone who deals with allegations and suspicions of abuse maintains an open and inquiring mind. Although there is an obvious need to act with speed and decisiveness in cases where there is reasonable cause for suspicion that a child may be in acute physical danger, the potential for damage to the long-term future of the child by precipitate action must always be considered. There must be confidence that agencies will act in a careful measured way when suspicions are brought to their attention.

STRUCTURE OF THIS DOCUMENT

1.14 This document is not intended to be a practice guide for any particular agency or worker. It provides:

- advice on the role of the Area Child Protection Committee;
- a brief account of some of the legal and ethical considerations which underpin work in child protection;
- an overview of the roles and organisation and arrangements of the major agencies engaged in child protection work;
- advice on working together in individual cases;
- advice on the function and operation of child protection conferences and registers;
- advice on training in child protection work;
- advice on reviewing cases.

PART 2

AREA CHILD PROTECTION COMMITTEES

INTRODUCTION

2.1 Inter-disciplinary and inter-agency work is an essential process in the task of attempting to protect children from abuse. Local systems for inter-agency co-operation have been set up throughout England and Wales. The experience gained by professionals in working and training together has succeeded in bringing about a greater mutual understanding of the roles of the various professions and agencies and a greater ability to combine their skills in the interest of abused children and their families.

2.2 Much has been achieved. However, co-operation and collaboration between different agencies is a difficult and complex process, particularly in an area of work like child protection in which policy and practice are constantly developing to absorb new ideas acquired through experience, research and innovative practice. All agencies concerned with the care of children are aware of the need to adapt and change in response to the growth of knowledge and understanding, and they must all share the responsibility for establishing and maintaining close working arrangements for all types of cases involving the protection of children.

2.3 For each agency, chief officers and authority members as appropriate must take responsibility for establishing and maintaining the inter-agency arrangements and should assure themselves from time to time that appropriate arrangements are in place. In the case of the National Health Service, this responsibility rests with the regional as well as the district authorities.

METHOD OF ACHIEVING JOINT POLICIES

2.4 In every local authority area there is a need for a close working relationship between social services departments, the police service, medical practitioners, community health workers, the education service and others who share a common aim to protect the child at risk. Co-operation at the individual case level needs to be supported by joint agency and management policies for child protection, consistent with their policies and plans for related service provision. There needs to be a recognised joint forum for developing, monitoring and reviewing child protection policies. This forum is the Area Child Protection Committee (ACPC).

2.5 To be fully effective a joint forum needs to have a clearly recognised relationship to the responsible agencies. Generally, one ACPC should cover one local authority and all the police or district health authorities or parts of them within that local authority boundary.

2.6 The following paragraphs make recommendations about accountability, organisation, funding, management information and reporting systems to assist the effective operation of ACPCs and improve their accountability.

ACCOUNTABILITY

2.7 ACPC members are accountable to the agencies which they represent. These agencies are jointly responsible for ACPC actions. Each ACPC should have a clearly defined and agreed relationship with its constituent agencies and the individual agencies should endorse the policies, procedures and actions of the ACPC.

REPRESENTATION AND DECISION MAKING

2.8 All agencies should recognise the importance of securing effective co-operation by appointing senior officers to the ACPC. Their appointees should have sufficient authority to allow them to speak on their agencies' behalf and to make decisions to an agreed level without referral to the appointees' agencies. The level of decision making delegated to appointees needs to be considerable to enable ACPCs to operate effectively. ACPC members will be senior officers or senior professionals from all the main authorities and agencies in the area which are involved in the prevention and management of child abuse. Detailed recommendations on the membership of ACPCs are provided in Appendix 5. The local authority has a responsibility to ensure that adequate legal advice is made available to the ACPC.

CHAIR AND SECRETARIAT

2.9 The lead responsibility for the appointment of the Chair and the secretariat and support services for the Committee should rest with the social services department. Where the Chair is an officer of the social services department, the individual should be of at least Assistant Director status and should possess knowledge and experience of child protection work in addition to chairing skills. However, there will be situations where the social services department, with the agreement of the heads of the other agencies concerned, arranges for the Chair to be taken on its behalf by a senior officer of one of the other agencies, or by an independent person with the requisite knowledge, experience and chairing skills. In such a case, the Vice-Chair of the ACPC should be a senior officer of the social services department. The Director of the social services department should ensure that social services officers take the lead in monitoring implementation of the local procedures and the efficacy of arrangements and in securing legal advice for the ACPC.

RESPONSIBILITIES OF THE ACPC

2.10 The ACPC should work to agreed written terms of reference which set out the remit of the ACPC and the level of decision which may be agreed by agencies' representatives without referral back to individual member agencies.

2.11 Each agency should accept that it is responsible for monitoring the performance of its own representative. Each agency must have procedures for considering reports from its ACPC representative to identify any action necessary within the agency or the ACPC. Decisions which have implications for policy, planning and resources need to be reported on and discussed at appropriate levels within agencies.

MAIN TASKS OF THE ACPC

2.12 Each ACPC should establish a programme of work to develop and keep under review local joint working and policies and procedures. The main tasks of the ACPC will be:

(a) to establish, maintain and review local inter-agency guidelines on procedures to be followed in individual cases;

(b) to monitor the implementation of legal procedures;

(c) to identify significant issues arising from the handling of cases and reports from inquiries;

(d) to scrutinise arrangements to provide treatment, expert advice and inter-agency liaison and make recommendations to the responsible agencies;

(e) to scrutinise progress on work to prevent child abuse and make recommendations to the responsible agencies;

(f) to scrutinise work related to inter-agency training and make recommendations to the responsible agencies;

(g) to conduct reviews required under Part 8 of this Guide;

(h) to publish an annual report about local child protection matters.

WORKING GROUPS

2.13 Where the boundaries of agencies and authorities are not coterminous, and where a wide variety of agencies and professionals are represented on an ACPC, this can lead to a large and unwieldy committee. Experience has shown that some of the tasks of policy formulation can effectively be delegated to a smaller group within the ACPC, representing the key agencies in the area, reporting back to the full committee.

2.14 Some ACPCs have the practice of co-opting key professionals for particular purposes, or of establishing standing sub-committees to help undertake the work of the ACPC. Where ACPCs have established standing sub-committees, they have usually been in the following categories:

(1) *groups commissioned by the ACPC to carry out specific tasks*. Examples of such tasks are: to oversee local procedures; to provide a training programme; to review cases under Part 8 of this Guide; to review the work on a selection of routine cases known to the child protection agencies; and to make proposals for a programme of work with abusers;

(2) *groups to provide specialist advice to the ACPC*. Examples are: advice on work with young abusers; advice on development of treatment services; advice in relation to specific ethnic and cultural groups;

(3) *groups which represent those providing local child protection services within a defined geographical area*. These can perform an important function in providing local information on which the ACPC can base its deliberations concerning policy and practice and also provide a mechanism to help ensure that the decisions and policies agreed by the ACPC are implemented consistently across the area.

2.15 All standing sub-committees, whatever their purpose, should have a defined membership, aims and objectives, clearly delineated tasks, and explicit lines of communication and accountability to the ACPC. Some standing sub-committees may be specific to particular groups of professions. There may be occasions when an ACPC wishes to set up an *ad hoc* committee. The same need to define purpose and accountability applies.

JOINT FINANCING AND EXPENSES

2.16 It will be the duty of the agencies represented on an ACPC to reach agreements on the budget the ACPC requires to accomplish the tasks which have been identified and in order to support the work of the secretariat. Agencies should allocate funds to the ACPC in accordance with agreed arrangements at the beginning of each financial year so that the ACPC has an annual budget. A member of the ACPC should be appointed, with the support of their agency, to act as the officer responsible for the budget. Joint financing by health and social services may be used for this purpose. When training is arranged on a multi-agency basis costs should be shared accordingly.

2.17 The ACPC will need to reach agreement as to the expenses that may be incurred by the Committee and its working groups, and to make such arrangements as may be agreed between them for the payment of such expenses. It is expected that each agency represented on an ACPC should defray the expenses of its representatives.

LOCAL PROCEDURAL HANDBOOKS

2.18 ACPCs should produce local procedural handbooks, derived from and consistent with this Guide. These handbooks should also be concerned mainly with inter-agency procedures, rather than with detailed professional practice. ACPCs should regularly re-examine and, where necessary, revise these handbooks so that they represent a comprehensive and up-to-date statement of local policy. A standard approach is recommended and an outline of the basic content and format is set out in Appendix 6. The documents should be available to the public, for instance through local libraries, and on special request, to individuals with, if necessary, an appropriate explanation of their purpose.

2.19 Local procedural handbooks should be accessible in constituent agencies to all members of staff, and to independent practitioners in direct contact with children and families, including independent schools, day care centres and appropriate local voluntary organisations.

REPORTS TO ACPCs

2.20 In order that the ACPC can carry out its functions, constituent agencies should make available to the ACPC, on a regular basis, management information on the level of activity on child abuse work, type and trends. The aim should be to produce this information quarterly. It should not include identifying details of individuals. Appendix 7 gives a suggested outline of the information to be provided by each agency.

REPORTS FROM ACPCs

2.21 Building on this information, each ACPC should reappraise annually the work which has been done locally to protect children from harm in its area and plan for the year ahead. The annual report of the ACPC, which should be made by the ACPC to the head of each agency, should underline that the accountability for the work of the ACPC rests with its constituent members. A recommended outline format for this report is shown in Appendix 8. A copy of the report should be sent to the Department of Health or Welsh Office Social Services Inspectorate and to the Regional Health Authority and to local JCCs for information, by the end of July each year. The Social Services Inspectorate will arrange for copies to be sent to Department of Health headquarters or Welsh Office, the Department of Education and Science, the Home Office and Her Majesty's Inspectorates of Constabulary and Schools as appropriate.

2.22 Extracts from the report could form the basis of local publicity to inform and involve the community at large in the work to protect children.

PART 3

SOME LEGAL AND ETHICAL CONSIDERATIONS

3.1 All agencies working in the area of child protection need to understand something of the legal and ethical constraints which govern workers in other agencies. This section needs to be read in the light of Appendix 2 and the volumes of Guidance and Regulations on the Children Act 1989 (in particular, volumes 1, 3 and 4).

3.2 Social services, which include the child care services, are provided by local authority social services departments. The social services department will operate in accordance with local authority policies, the legal framework and under the general guidance of the Secretary of State.

3.3 Child care legislation, which has as its main consideration the welfare of children, places upon local authority social services departments statutory duties in relation to children. These statutory duties impose a responsibility to investigate reports of children suffering, or likely to suffer, significant harm and to take appropriate action to safeguard or promote the child's welfare. These duties and responsibilities apply to all children whether the child is living at home with parents, in residential care in either a children's home or a residential school, or living with another carer (who may be a local authority foster carer).

3.4 Local authorities also have a duty to provide services to prevent children in their area suffering ill treatment or neglect and to reduce the need to bring court proceedings in respect of them. These combine with a general duty to safeguard and promote the welfare of children in need in their area and so far as is consistent with that to promote their upbringing by their families.

3.5 The primary responsibility of the social services department in relation to child care and protection does not diminish the role of other agencies or the need for inter-agency co-operation in the planning and provision of services for a child or family. In particular, the duty of education authorities, housing authorities and health authorities to co-operate with the lead social services authority in the exercise of their functions to support children and families is set out in Section 27 of the Children Act 1989. A fuller explanation of the duties and requirements of the Children Act is set out in the guidance published by the Department of Health. A summary is shown in Appendix 2.

INVESTIGATION OF ABUSE AND NEGLECT

Section 37 Children Act 1989
Section 47(1) Children Act 1989
Section 47(8) Children Act 1989
Schedule 2, paragraph 4, Children Act 1989

3.6 Local authorities have a statutory duty to investigate where they have reasonable cause to suspect that a child is suffering, or is likely to suffer, significant harm and to assess the needs of the child and the family including the likelihood of significant harm and the need for protection. The investigative process should involve gathering information from other key professionals, and liaising with other investigating agencies (e.g. police, NSPCC). The statutory duties and responsibilities of the local authority should be made clear to everyone at the outset. The local authority should decide what, if any, action is necessary to protect the child, e.g. protection in the family (or wider family), or placement outside the family. Any action should be taken in collaboration with the other agencies involved, whether the child is living at home, with foster carers, in a residential home or school or in any other situation. If the child moves to another area, that local authority must be told and a decision reached quickly about any action which is needed and who will carry out the action.

3.7 Although the police will wish to ensure that all appropriate steps are taken for the protection of the child, the primary responsibility for this will fall to the social services department. Because the functions of each agency are different in the investigation of an allegation of child abuse it is essential that methods of joint working are established, agreed and promulgated in the local ACPC procedural handbook. This should cover consultation, how enquiries will be pursued and the arrangements for obtaining court orders and removing the child if necessary.

REMOVAL OF CHILDREN FROM HOME

3.8 The removal of children from their home gives rise to public and professional concern, causes great distress if not handled sensitively, and can be damaging both for the child and for the rest of the family. Therefore, **except when a child is in acute physical danger it is essential that the timing of the removal of children from their homes should be agreed following consultation with all appropriate professionals**. They should weigh up the likely immediate and long term effects of removing the child against the possibility of harm if they leave the child at home, and balance this with the need to secure evidence of criminal offences and, in some cases, to arrest the suspects. In many cases there will be no need to remove a child and simultaneously arrest a suspect living in the same home. In other cases, however, particularly those involving several children and adults in different households, it may be important to prevent suspects from communicating with each other or destroying evidence. In those cases it may be necessary for co-ordinated police action, distressing though this may be, at a time of day when the whole family is at home. In other cases, although early morning police action might secure better forensic evidence, such action may not be crucial to the overall welfare of the child(ren) and should not therefore be part of the plan for investigation. In all cases, the long term protection of and well-being of the child will be the overriding concern; the likelihood of securing the child's well-being through the courts will be an important consideration.

SOME OTHER LEGISLATIVE PROVISIONS

3.9 A number of other recent legislative provisions have implications for child protection work. It is important that professionals understand the legislative framework within which colleagues work. This document is not intended to enable all professionals to take on the roles of other professions, nor is that the intention of joint working. It is important that professionals understand the constraints and context in which their colleagues work. The main provisions are:

The Criminal Justice Act 1988, as amended by the 1991 Act, which makes substantial changes to the way in which children's evidence may be received by the courts in criminal proceedings. The Act will allow a video recording of an interview with a child to be used as the child's main evidence in criminal proceedings subject to certain conditions. The Home Office is preparing a Code of Practice which will provide specific guidance on how to produce a video for this purpose. This guidance will cover essential technical advice, as well as legal and child welfare issues. Agencies using video recordings as part of their work with children should develop local procedures for recording in line with the forthcoming Code of Practice. Training in the use of video technology needs to be considered by the ACPC, and advice on this will be forthcoming.

The Police and Criminal Evidence Act 1984 (PACE) sets out the main powers of the police to investigate criminal offences. It also makes provision for the protection of the suspect's rights. The Act is wide-ranging and covers such areas as police powers to stop, search, arrest and detain. Five statutory codes of practice make more detailed provision for the observance of the Act and the most relevant of these is Code C, which deals with the detention, treatment and questioning of persons in police custody. It includes guidance on the treatment of juvenile suspects and the administration of caution.

The Prohibition of Female Circumcision Act 1985 makes female circumcision, excision and infibulation ("female genital mutilation") an offence except on specific physical and mental health grounds. If a local authority has reason to believe that a child is likely to suffer significant harm as a result of female circumcision, it should consider to what extent it should exercise its investigative powers under Section 47 of the Children Act 1989. In areas where there are significant numbers of children of particular ethnic minority or cultural backgrounds, workers will need to be alert to the possibility of female circumcision. Advice on this matter can be obtained from the Foundation for Womens Health Research and Development (FORWARD) at the Africa Centre in London, or from the School of Oriental and African Studies, University of London.

The Access to Personal Files Act 1987 and **The Access to Personal Files (Social Services) Regulations 1989** (S.I.1989/206) deal with client access to manually kept social work records. Guidance to local authorities on this is given in LAC(89)2. Local authorities should ensure that other agencies are aware of the implications of this legislation.

The Data Protection Act 1984 and **The Data Protection (Subject Access Modification) (Social Work) Order 1987 (S.I. 1987/1904)** and **The Data Protection (Subject Access Modification) (Health) Order 1987 (S.I. 1987/1903)** deal with computer-held records. Guidance is given in LAC(87)10 and LAC(88)16 respectively.

The Access to Health Records Act 1990 gives individuals the right of access to recorded health information about themselves which is not already covered by rights of access to computerised records under the Data Protection Act 1984. The Act sets out in Section 5(1) three cases where access is not to be given to the whole of a health record.

(a) The first is the case where, in the opinion of the holder of the record, giving access would disclose information likely to cause serious harm to the physical or mental health of the patient or of any other individual.

(b) The second is where giving access would, in the opinion of the holder of the record, disclose information relating to or provided by an individual other than the patient who could be identified from that information.

(c) The third is where the relevant part of a health record was made before the commencement of the Act on 1 November 1991. Guidance is contained in HSG(91)6.

The Education (School Records) Regulations 1989 (S.I. 1989/1261). These concern the keeping, disclosure and transfer of educational records of pupils maintained manually by schools. The principal objective is to allow parents and older pupils to have access to them on request but the Regulations do not authorise or require the disclosure to them of any information relating to child protection.

EXCHANGE OF INFORMATION

3.10 Arrangements for the protection of children from abuse, and in particular child protection conferences, can only be successful if the professional staff concerned do all they can to work in partnership and share and exchange relevant information, in particular with social services departments (or the NSPCC) and the police. Those in receipt of information from professional colleagues in this context must treat it as having been given in confidence. They must not disclose such information for any other purpose without consulting the person who provided it.

3.11 Ethical and statutory codes concerned with confidentiality and data protection are not intended to prevent the exchange of information between different professional staff who have a responsibility for ensuring the protection of children. These statements were drawn up with general considerations in mind. The field of child protection is an area which is developing and professionals should recognise that they may need to seek clarification from their professional body in particular cases.

Medical

3.12 The Annual Report 1987 of the General Medical Council gives unequivocal advice on this matter in cases of child abuse, including child sexual abuse:

"The Council's published guidance on professional confidence states that doctors may disclose confidential information to the police who are investigating a grave or very serious crime, provided always that they are prepared to justify their actions if called upon to do so. However, a specialist in child psychiatry recently drew to the Council's attention that its guidance does not specifically address the question of whether a doctor may properly initiate action in a case of this kind, as opposed to responding to a request. Both the British Medical Association and the medical defence societies have expressed the view that in such circumstances the interests of the child are paramount and that those interests may well override the general rule of professional confidence. On the recommendation of the Standards Committee, the Council in November 1987 expressed the view that, if a doctor has reason for believing that a child is being physically or sexually abused, not only is it permissible for the doctor to disclose information to a third party but it is a duty of the doctor to do so."

This is still the stance of the General Medical Council.

Nursing

3.13 The United Kingdom Central Council for Nursing, Midwifery and Health Visiting published a UKCC Advisory Paper on Confidentiality in April 1987. This states:

"In all cases where the practitioner deliberately discloses or withholds information in what he/she believes is the public interest he/she must be able to justify the decision. These situations can be particularly stressful, especially where vulnerable groups are concerned, as disclosure may mean the involvement of a third party as in the case of children or the mentally handicapped. **Practitioners should always take the opportunity to disuss the matter fully with other practitioners** (not only or necessarily fellow nurses, midwives and health visitors), and if appropriate consult with a professional organisation before making a decision. There will often be ramifications and these are best explored before a final decision as to whether to withhold or disclose information is made."

Social Work

3.14 A Code of Ethics for Social Work adopted by the British Association of Social Workers in 1986 states as a principle of practice:

"They will recognise that information clearly entrusted for one purpose should not be used for another purpose without sanction. They will respect the privacy of clients and others with whom they come into contact and confidential information gained in their relationships with them. They will divulge such information only with the consent of the client (or informant) except where there is clear evidence of serious danger to the client, worker, other persons or the community or in other circumstances judged exceptional, on the basis of professional consideration and consultation."

3.15 In child protection work the degree of confidentiality will be governed by the need to protect the child. Social workers and others working with a child and family must make clear to those providing information that confidentiality may not be maintained if the withholding of the information will prejudice the welfare of a child. Department of Health guidance to social services departments on the confidentiality and disclosure of personal information is contained in LAC(88)17 "Personal Social Services: Confidentiality of Personal Information".

RECORDS

3.16 Staff in different agencies, and other practitioners, will maintain their own records of the case and such records should be subject to the arrangements for maintaining confidentiality within that particular agency. Well-kept records are essential to good child protection practice and each agency should have a policy stating the purpose and the format for keeping records; this should cover the need to retain records for appropriate periods. All agencies must establish procedures to safeguard information provided to them and to ensure timely transfer of relevant records when a child and/or family moves to or from an area.

CRIMINAL PROCEEDINGS: EVIDENCE

3.17 Section 97 of the Children Act 1989 is intended to ensure that relevant evidence is brought before the court in care and related proceedings under Parts IV and V of the Act. A statement or admission which may incriminate a person or his or her spouse and which is given in the course of such proceedings cannot be used in evidence against the person making it or his or her spouse in proceedings for an offence other than perjury. Accordingly, no person is excused from giving evidence of this nature on the basis that it might incriminate themselves or their spouse.

PART 4   ROLE OF AGENCIES INVOLVED IN CHILD PROTECTION

4.1 This section deals with the roles of agencies and other associated groups in relation to child protection and how their duties and functions should be organised in order to contribute to inter-agency co-operation for the protection of children. Although the subsequent paragraphs relate specifically to the duties of particular professions or groups, this section should be read in the context of the document as a whole. The responsibility for protecting children should not fall entirely to one agency: awareness and appreciation of another agency's role will contribute greatly to collaborative practices.

SOCIAL SERVICES

4.2 Social services departments have a wide range of duties and responsibilities to provide services for individuals and for families. The services which they are required to provide encompass people of all ages, abilities and social groupings. Social services departments provide services for people living in the community in their own homes and they also provide residential and day care services. In addition they have regulatory functions in relation to services provided by the voluntary and private sector and they may also work collaboratively with these bodies.

4.3 The child protection work of social services departments should be considered in the wider context of all the department's work and more precisely in the context of its child care services. Field workers engaged in child protection work are also involved in a wide range of other child care work and they often work with other client groups. They are aware of the wider child care facilities provided and known to the department and can draw on these in order to provide support and treatment services for children who have been abused. These include day care facilities, residential accommodation and foster homes.

4.4 Local authorities are under a statutory duty to investigate where they have reasonable cause to suspect that a child is or is likely to suffer significant harm or is subject to an emergency protection order or police protection. The social services department carries these responsibilities on behalf of the local authority. They do not do this alone and of necessity call on the expertise and knowledge of other agencies and professionals. Part 5 of this Guide outlines the process for handling individual cases from referral and investigation through the child protection process to removal of the child's name from the child protection register; this section illustrates how the social services department takes the lead role in managing individual cases but also relies on the assistance and co-operation of professionals in other agencies. The social services department also carries responsibilities for managing key parts of the child protection service such as child protection conferences and the child protection register.

4.5 Many staff involved in child protection work need access to specialist advice. Some social services departments have designated an individual or individuals who can offer this kind of advice. This role may be combined with responsibility for management of the child protection register. The creation of such posts which provide specialist advice, however designated, has proved successful and is commended.

4.6 The senior managers and practitioners of the social services department contribute to the work of the Area Child Protection Committee and work with colleagues from other child protection agencies in planning and promoting good child protection services.

4.7 Social services departments should ensure that they have effective arrangements to allow members of the public to refer to them their concern about individual children. The size and complexities of social services departments can make it difficult for members of the public to know how to contact relevant personnel. Social services departments should publicise widely a telephone number which can be used by people concerned about a child and by children themselves. Sites for publicity could include public libraries, health clinics, community centres, general medical practitioners' waiting rooms and other suitable local premises.

GUARDIANS AD LITEM AND REPORTING OFFICERS

4.8 The guardian ad litem and reporting officer service provides independent social work advice to courts aimed at safeguarding and promoting the interests of the child in care, adoption and related proceedings. Since 1984 the courts have been required to appoint guardians ad litem (GALs) from panels established by local authorities in accordance with Regulations made under the Children Act 1975. Under the Children Act 1989 the GAL's role will be enhanced – there is a presumption in favour of appointing a GAL in a wider range of proceedings in the High Court, County Courts and Magistrates' Courts. They have an important role in assisting the courts to take a proactive stance with regard to the conduct of proceedings and the range of possible orders and powers which the Act requires. GALs will be appointed earlier in the proceedings so that they can play a full and active role in advising the court on issues of case management, and in helping with the formulation of any directions on assessment at the interim or emergency stage.

4.9 Since their duty is to represent the interests of the child in court proceedings, it should be exceptional for GALs to take part in child protection except in the case of a child protection conference following an application for an emergency protection order (EPO), or interim care order, when it might be helpful for them to be present as part of the process of gathering information for the court. The GAL would be present as an observer, not a participant, given his/her position as an officer of the court.

4.10 All agencies should be aware that GALs have a right of access to local authority records concerning a child under Section 42 of the Children Act 1989.

THE POLICE

4.11 Police involvement in cases of child abuse stems from their primary responsibilities to protect the community and to bring offenders to justice. Their overriding consideration is the welfare of the child. In the spirit of *Working Together*, the police focus will be to determine whether a criminal offence has been committed, to identify the person or persons responsible and to secure the best possible evidence in order that appropriate consideration can be given as to whether criminal proceedings should be instituted. Failure to conduct child abuse investigations in the most effective manner may mean that the best possible protection cannot be provided for a child victim.

4.12 The decision whether or not criminal proceedings should be initiated will be based on three main factors: whether or not there is sufficient substantial evidence to prosecute; whether it is in the public interest that proceedings should be instigated against a particular offender; and whether or not it is in the interests of the child victim that proceedings should be instituted. Although the police may instigate proceedings it is the responsibility of the Crown Prosecution Service to review and, where appropriate, conduct all criminal proceedings instigated on behalf of a police service. In some cases advice from the Crown Prosecution Service will be sought prior to proceedings being instituted.

4.13 The evidential requirement of the criminal courts is proof beyond reasonable doubt that the defendant committed the offence of which he/she stands indicted. The burden of proof rests with the prosecution, i.e. the defendant does not have to prove his innocence. Proceedings for the protection of children under the Children Act take place in the civil courts which work to a lesser standard of proof, that of the balance of probabilities. It is not unusual for the police or the Crown Prosecution Service to decide that criminal proceedings cannot be instigated against a person suspected of child abuse on the grounds that there is insufficient evidence to meet the higher standard of proof and for the civil courts to decide that the child needs protection from the same individual. The criminal courts focus on the behaviour of the *defendant*; the civil courts on the interest of the *child*.

4.14 In investigating an allegation of child abuse the police will normally collect a considerable amount of information. Irrespective of their decision whether or not to institute criminal proceedings, the information they hold may be highly relevant to a decision about a child who may need protection from abuse, and should, where appropriate, be shared with other agencies.

4.15 As indicated in Appendix 2, the police have an emergency power, which is not available to other agencies, to detain a child in a place of protection without prior application to a court. They can obtain a warrant under Section 102 of the Children Act to enter premises and search for children. Where speed is essential to protect a child and a warrant would take too long to obtain they can also act without it to enter premises in order to save life and limb under Section 17(1)(e) of the Police and Criminal Evidence Act 1984.

Police/Social Services Consultation

4.16 Although in cases of child abuse both the police and social services have as their foremost objective the welfare of the child, their primary functions, powers and methods of working are different. Whilst the police will focus on the investigation of alleged offences, the social services are concerned with the welfare of the child and other members of the family.

4.17 Difficulties will be encountered in joint inter-agency investigations but these can be minimised by the selection of specialist staff who undergo appropriate inter-agency training. However, it is essential that methods of joint working are established between the two agencies over and above the joint interviewing of child victims. There should be agreed procedures for the joint inter-agency investigation process which ensure that there is adequate planning and full consultation at all stages of any investigation. It is important that those engaged in child abuse investigation and their supervisors fully understand the responsibilities of both agencies, the powers available to them and the different standards of proof that exist in relation to criminal and civil proceedings. This will assist to remove some of the tensions that can otherwise exist.

HEALTH SERVICES

4.18 All those working in the field of health have a commitment to protect children, and their participation in inter-agency support to social services departments is essential if the interests of children are to be safeguarded. Health professionals are major contributors to the inter-agency care of children which extends beyond the initial referral and assessment, into child protection conference attendance, participation in planning and the ongoing support of the child and family. There will always be a need for close co-operation with other agencies, including any other health professionals involved.

District Health Authority

4.19 A health authority must comply with a request for help from a local authority provided that the request is compatible with its own statutory or other duties and does not unduly prejudice the discharge of its function (Section 27 of the Children Act).

4.20 Each health authority should identify a senior doctor, a senior nurse with a health visiting qualification and a senior midwife (designated senior professional) as the co-ordinator of all aspects of child protection work within their district. This will include the provision of advice to social services departments and to health professionals. (See the glossary for the role of the designated senior professional.) The commissioning authority should ensure that child protection is included in the contracts that they agree with providers and that monitoring arrangements are set up. The role of the designated senior professional is vital to the protection of children. The designated senior professional should take responsibility for identifying the training needs of their professional groups in child protection procedures. All training will include an element of clinical instruction.

4.21 The co-ordinating role should ensure the effective contribution from health service personnel involved with the child and family, for example facilitating attendance at child protection conferences and ensuring that the follow up work necessary to promote the child's health and development is carried out. The co-ordinating role of the designated senior professional should extend beyond doctors and nurses (including community psychiatric nurses and midwives) to other health service personnel involved in the care of children including, for example, physiotherapists, occupational therapists, speech therapists and clinical psychologists.

4.22 It is of great importance that all health professionals keep meticulous records and, with due regard to confidentiality, they should be prepared to share the information contained in them with others who need to know including carers and children.

The Role of the Midwife and Health Visitor

4.23 During pregnancy and birth and the early care of children, parents will be in contact with the maternity and child health services, and this offers opportunities for the preparation and support of parents in the care of children. Medical, nursing and midwifery staff have a part to play, but the major roles are played by the midwife and health visitor working together. Parents are responsible for the well-being and protection of their children. The encouragement to take a responsible attitude to the care of their children and to seek appropriate help and support will do much to prevent child abuse. Child abuse is less likely if there is an affectionate and positive relationship between parents and baby. The need to promote this, particularly when babies have had to spend some time in hospital after birth, was emphasised in the Third Report of the Maternity Services Advisory Committee published in 1985 which remains government policy. In Wales guidance has been issued under WHC(86)69. The midwife or the health visitor caring for the mother during the antenatal period may be concerned about the future welfare of the unborn child and may believe there is a need for a protection plan to be considered. In such circumstances the social services department should be notified and consideration given to holding a pre-birth child protection conference.

All Hospital Staff

4.24 Staff in hospital departments see children in the course of their normal duties and need to be alert to indications of child abuse. Abused children may attend hospital accident and emergency departments as a consequence of injuries inflicted on them. All hospital staff, whether working in directly managed units or in NHS Trusts, should be alert to carers who may shop around for medical services in order to conceal the repeated nature of their child's injuries. All hospital staff must, therefore, be familiar with local procedures for checking the child protection register, and should develop good working relations with the hospital social services departments and district social services departments, so that good inter-agency working can operate at all times. Advice and assistance should be sought on procedural matters from the designated senior professional for child protection. There will be occasions when additional clinical advice will be needed, and in these situations help should be sought from the appropriate clinical specialist in determining the exact significance of the history of injuries. Arrangements should be made to notify the health visitor or school nurse of all visits made by children aged 0–16 years to the accident and emergency department. Notification of all visits made by children to accident and emergency departments should also be made to the GP and all delays in the passage of information should be minimised.

Primary and Community Health Services

4.25 Health surveillance programmes are a well-recognised part of the primary services for children. Parents are encouraged to bring their children to child health clinics where health visitors and doctors will be involved in monitoring the child's health and development. Traditionally these services have been provided by the Health Authority, but general medical practitioners, in conjunction with health visitors, are becoming increasingly involved. Children are brought to the clinic or the general practitioner for immunisations and at other times for routine screening and surveillance. Domiciliary visits may be made in situations where this is judged to be helpful to the family, for example travelling families, those in temporary accommodation, and especially those who do not readily take up the services offered. Similarly, school nurses and school doctors will be involved in monitoring the child's health and development after he or she has started school. These and other community health staff are well placed to identify children who are being harmed or who may be at risk of harm and should be aware of the signs and symptoms of abuse, and the procedures to follow. All staff should be alert to the needs of children and to factors which may affect them adversely.

4.26 In accordance with policies agreed between District Health Authorities and Family Health Service Authorities (FHSAs) and general practitioners, the community child health service offers screening and surveillance. In carrying out this role staff will be well placed to identify children who may be or who are being abused. The community child health service offers in addition a specialist service for children who may be or who have been abused. Community child health staff, under the direction of a consultant community paediatrician or the lead senior clinical medical officer, are uniquely placed to develop a high level of expertise in the examination, diagnosis, assessment and ongoing care of abused children. It is likely that the designated senior doctor with responsibility for co-ordinating the provision of advice to social services and other duties described in the glossary will be a community child health doctor.

Child and Adolescent Mental Health Service

4.27 In the course of their work those involved in this service may identify or come to suspect the presence of abuse. The staff will need to be fully conversant with the child protection procedures outlined for their district. The service will already have established links with the statutory agencies holding responsibility for child protection, which will help in rapid notification and in formulating a planned inter-agency management programme.

4.28 The service will receive requests for assessment and/or treatment for families in which abuse is an issue from various sources including the child or parent, as well as a statutory agency. The service will need to focus on the needs of the child and on those of the parents. Where there is a conflict between those needs, the child's needs must be the foremost consideration. Other services may need to be approached or the child and adolescent mental health service may be able to work with the family to resolve the conflict.

4.29 The Child and Adolescent Mental Health Service may also have a role in assessing and treating the abuser, especially if the abuser is a child or adolescent. When the abuser is a member of the family, the discovery of causative factors can provide knowledge useful in preventing further abuse in other families at risk. This service may need to liaise with the Adult Psychiatric Service if the abuser is already known to them in order to instigate joint work, and with other services providing treatment programmes for sex offenders, where the abuse has been sexual abuse.

Family Health Service Authorities

4.30 Family Health Service Authorities (FHSAs) have an important role in relation to their contractors, particularly general medical practitioners, in keeping them informed about child protection matters. Each FHSA should identify a named person to co-ordinate the provision of advice to social services departments and to advise their contractors (including dentists, opticians and pharmacists). In collaboration with other agencies they should ensure that local arrangements, for example on the timing of child protection conferences, are such that the contribution of GPs can be brought to bear effectively. They should also contribute to the monitoring of these arrangements. FHSAs should be aware of the continuous role GPs have in the care of children and families in relation to child protection issues. FHSAs should encourage GPs to receive training in child protection whilst Regional advisers in general practice have a role to play in encouraging and enabling GPs to receive training in all aspects of child protection matters.

General Practitioners

4.31 General practitioners have a vital role to play in the protection of children. As family doctors, working closely with health visitors, and other members of the primary health care team, they are well placed to identify at an early stage family stress which may point to a risk of child abuse, or to notice in the child indications of significant harm, or likelihood of significant harm. As more general practitioners become involved in child health surveillance programmes their role in preventing child abuse and in protecting children will increase. General practitioners' extensive knowledge of the family background enables them to make a particular contribution to child protection conferences and to the long term support of the child and family. While general practitioners have responsibilities to all their patients the protection of the child is paramount.

4.32 It is essential that whenever a general practitioner becomes suspicious that a child may be at risk of, or is the subject of abuse of whatever nature, the information is shared with the statutory services responsible for child protection, i.e. social services departments, the NSPCC or the police. In addition concerns may need to be discussed with colleagues experienced in working with child abuse cases where there is clinical uncertainty. General practitioners should ensure that practice nurses receive appropriate training in the recognition of child abuse and in the operation of local procedures. Practice nurses should have clearly defined professional support and clinical supervision.

Private Health Care

4.33 All health professionals who work in private health care must be aware of their duties to protect children and should know about the child protection procedures of the health authority in whose district they are based. Doctors, nurses and other professionals who see children and their families on a private basis must follow the appropriate child protection procedure if they become suspicious about a child's care.

4.34 Probation officers may become involved in cases of child abuse as a result either of their responsibility for the supervision of offenders, including those convicted of offences against children, or of their responsibility to the court for the supervision of children following marital breakdown. They may be able to identify potential cases and bring in other agencies when, through their work, they become concerned about the safety of a child. Arrangements exist to ensure that when offenders convicted of offences against children are discharged from prison, probation services inform the local authority in the area in which the discharged prisoner plans to reside. This allows the social services department to make inquiries and take action if they believe there may be danger to children residing at the same address.

THE EDUCATION SERVICE

4.35 The education service does not constitute an investigation or intervention agency, but has an important role to play at the recognition and referral stage. Because of their day-to-day contact with individual children during school terms, teachers and other school staff are particularly well placed to observe outward signs of abuse, changes in behaviour or failure to develop. Education welfare officers and educational psychologists also have important roles because of their concern for the welfare and development of children. Youth workers have regular contact with some children, and will therefore also be in a position to help.

4.36 All staff in the education service – including those in grant maintained and independent schools, sixth form and further education colleges, and the youth service – should be aware of the need to alert the social services, the NSPCC or the police, when they believe a child has been abused or is at risk of abuse. They should refer cases according to the locally established procedures. For the institutions they maintain, local education authorities (LEAs) should seek to ensure that all staff are aware of this and know what the proper procedures are. Social services departments (SSDs) should ensure that educational establishments not maintained by the LEA are aware of the local inter-agency procedures, and the governing bodies/proprietors of these establishments should ensure that appropriate procedures are in place, seeking advice as necessary from the SSD. For all educational establishments, the procedures should cover circumstances where a member of staff is accused or suspected of abuse.

4.37 The key element essential to ensuring that proper procedures are followed in each educational establishment is that the headteacher or another senior member of staff should be designated as having responsibility for liaising with SSDs and other relevant agencies over cases of child abuse. For establishments maintained by them, LEAs should keep up-to-date lists of designated staff and ensure that these staff receive appropriate training and support.

4.38 The relevant school, including nursery school, should be promptly notified by the social services department of the inclusion of a child's name on the child protection register. The details notified should include the care status and placement of the child, the name of the key worker and where possible what information has been made known to the parents about any allegations or suspicions of abuse. Schools will wish to pay particular attention to the attendance and development of such children and the designated teacher should report any cause for further concern to the social services department. The social services department should inform the school of any decision to remove the child from the child protection register and of termination of a care order as well as any change in the status or the placement of the child. The social services department should inform the school when a child who is already on the child protection register starts school. When a child on the child protection register changes school, the information should be transferred between schools immediately and the custodian of the child protection register informed.

4.39 Schools and further education colleges have a role in preventing abuse not only by adopting sound policies and procedures on the management of situations where there is suspected abuse, but also through the curriculum. They can help pupils and students to acquire relevant information, skills and attitudes both to resist abuse in their own lives and to prepare them for the responsibilities of their adult lives, including parenthood. Some schools include specific teaching about the risks of child abuse and how pupils can protect themselves, within their personal and social education programmes.

4.40 A number of publications relating to health education and the development of a personal and social education curriculum are already available in schools and address issues related to child protection. More recently, the National Curriculum Council has advised that children aged five years and above should begin to develop skills and practices which will help them to maintain personal safety. It has also identified family life, sex and safety education as three key components of school health education, and has included family life education as a key topic in its advice to schools on education for citizenship. Its guidance to schools on both health and citizenship suggests ways in which these issues can be integrated into the wider curriculum and topics appropriate to different key stages.

DAY CARE SERVICES

4.41 Day nurseries, playgroups, out of school clubs and holiday schemes, and childminders, are likely to have an important part to play in helping parents under stress cope with their children's behaviour, to support them and give them a respite and thus prevent abuse. Local authorities will wish to ensure that all those providing such services and childminders are informed about what to do if they are concerned about a child. This should involve awareness training so that staff can recognise at an early stage the signs and behaviour which are a cause for concern. Day care providers in the private and voluntary sectors must have agreed procedures for contacting the local authority social services department about an individual child. In all cases the decision to contact the social services department should be made by a senior member of staff, normally the officer in charge or his or her deputy. Local authority provision will have its own procedures.

4.42 Day care services and those provided by childminders are also crucial services for children who are at risk. By helping children directly and by monitoring their care at home, these services may well be essential in helping a family remain together. Many local authority managed day nurseries have considerable experience of working with families where a child is in need of protection and some authorities have developed sponsored or salaried childminding schemes for them. Out of school services are generally less well developed across the country as a whole, but nevertheless some have been used for children in need of protection. It is important that people working in day care services or as childminders are properly supported and are enabled to contribute to child protection conferences and to the work of ACPCs where appropriate.

ARMED SERVICES

4.43 The life of a Service family differs in many respects from that of a family in civilian life. Although in England and Wales it is local authorities which have the primary responsibility for the care and protection of children, it is essential for the local authorities and other agencies to note these differences and share information with the Service authority when a Service family becomes the subject of a child abuse investigation. Unlike civilian life, responsibility for the welfare of Services families is invested in the employing service and specifically in the commanding officer. Service authorities are responsible for the housing of the family, their welfare support and for the medical services for Service personnel. They control the movement of the family in relation to Service commitments; the frequency of such moves makes it imperative that Service authorities are fully aware of any child who is deemed at risk. When Servicemen (or civilians working with the armed forces) are based overseas, the Service responsibility is widened to include the protection of their children. These arrangements and those for American Forces based in the United Kingdom are summarised in Appendix 3. It is essential that all agencies note these differences when a Service family becomes the subject of a child abuse investigation.

NATIONAL SOCIETY FOR THE PREVENTION OF CRUELTY TO CHILDREN (NSPCC)

4.44 Uniquely amongst voluntary bodies the NSPCC has a power to apply for care, supervision and child assessment orders in its own right. The NSPCC is a charitable organisation whose Royal Charter places upon it "the duty to ensure an appropriate and speedy response in all cases where children are alleged to be at risk of abuse or neglect in any form". Social workers employed by the NSPCC have a central concern to identify and prevent cruelty to children. Increasingly, the Society is creating, in co-operation with local authorities, child protection teams and projects to provide specialist services. The services provided by teams will vary according to local needs. Such collaboration is essential if the best use is to be made of the Society's expertise in child protection work. The NSPCC contributes to local and national training, particularly multi-disciplinary training. A child protection helpline has been established by the NSPCC for the use of all those who are concerned about children who may be abused or at risk, in particular, parents, relatives and the general public.

OTHER VOLUNTARY ORGANISATIONS

4.45 A wide range of voluntary organisations provide services, including telephone helplines, to help parents under stress and children at risk. Some of these are national, such as Childline, which provides counselling for children with problems; others are for the support of parents, such as Parentline, or are locally based. Authorities should be alert to the opportunities to promote voluntary effort in their area, and ensure that there is good liaison with voluntary organisations. Staff in these and other voluntary services concerned with children and families can also help by bringing children who are thought to be in need of protection to the attention of the statutory agencies. Voluntary organisations may have children in their care whom they have placed in foster or residential homes.

FAMILY COURT COMMITTEES

4.46 The Lord Chancellor's Department has set up a court committee structure to ensure the Children Act 1989 works as intended after implementation. Four levels of committee are involved: the national Children Act Advisory Committee; the annual Circuit Conferences; the Family Court Business Committees (FCBCs); and the Family Court Services Committees (FCSCs). Each of the 51 Care Centres will have an FCBC and an FCSC (apart from the Principal Registry of the Family Division, which has two FCBCs). Both the FCBCs and FCSCs will be chaired by the Designated Family Judge and serviced by the Courts Administrator. Part of their remit is to identify any necessary improvements to the service provided to the parties to family proceedings by the courts, or other agencies and professions. All agencies should be aware of the work of their Local Committees and prepared to contribute to it. They should also consider whether particular or general matters should be referred to the FCSC or FCBC for consideration.

4.47 The community as a whole has a responsibility for the well-being of children. This means that all citizens should remain alert to circumstances in which children may he harmed. Individuals can assist the statutory authorities by bringing cases to their attention. Relatives, friends and neighbours of children are particularly well placed to do so, but they must know what to do if they are concerned, in addition to providing support for the family and child, which may include help with caring for the child. They must also be confident, because of the difficult and sensitive nature of the situation, that any information they provide will be treated in a confidential way and used only to protect the interest of the child. They should know too that early action on their part is often the best way of helping a family stay together as well as protecting the child.

4.48 The availability locally of self-help groups, telephone helplines and other counselling services, often provided by volunteers, can do much to help parents help themselves or to seek help from others when it is needed. Victim support schemes which are being set up in many areas may be in a position to offer help to young people who have been abused.

PART 5

WORKING TOGETHER – INDIVIDUAL CASES

5.1 This section deals with the handling of individual cases. It is not a detailed practice guide. Its aim is to provide advice about the process which agencies should follow when working together to protect children. As with other sections of *Working Together*, those using Part 5 should refer to other guidance in the series concerned with the Children Act 1989.

5.2 There are a number of essential concepts which need to be accepted by all those who provide services under the inter-agency arrangements described in this Guide. The basis of an effective child protection service must be that professionals and individual agencies work together on a multi-disciplinary basis, with a shared mutual understanding of aims, of objectives and of what is good practice. This should take into account the sensitive issues associated with gender, race, culture and disability.

Court Action

5.3 While many cases, and it is hoped more than hitherto, will not need to be taken to court, the process of investigation, assessment and the provision of services to a child and family may need to run in parallel with court action: it is essential that the implications of this are borne in mind.

5.4 The essential principles of the Children Act provide the foundation for work on individual cases. They include:

- the focus on the welfare of the child taking account of the child's views in the light of age and his or her understanding;
- partnership with parents and other family members, and support of the child within the family whenever possible;
- the concept of parental responsibility.

5.5 Most child protection cases do not come before the courts. However, with the implementation of the Children Act in cases where there is a need for court intervention, the courts will be more involved in the handling of individual cases. Before the case is heard, there may be an initial hearing called a **directions appointment** at the court involving all those concerned with the case. This opportunity will be used to: give directions to everyone concerned about how the case should proceed; agree a timetable for the case; appoint a guardian ad litem to represent the child in court; decide whether the case should be transferred to another court; consider the attendance of the child; and give any other directions as appropriate, e.g. on contact and assessment. There are new arrangements for access to information. Everybody involved in the court proceedings should have access to the relevant information before the case is heard and will be expected to reveal their arguments and evidence in advance in writing to give everyone a chance to prepare their case. Emergency protection orders may be granted *ex parte*.

5.6 Working together requires its own skills and staff need to be competent in the ways of effective communication, co-ordination and co-operation. The process of working together combines the skills and expertise of a number of professionals. This group will include social worker, health visitor, child health doctor, general practitioner, police officer, and NSPCC. These disciplines are particularly involved in the process of gathering relevant information and carrying forward the work with a child and family. Sometimes others such as probation officers, teachers or psychiatrists will have an important role to play. On occasion they will need to supplement their own knowledge and expertise with specialist advice such as that provided by other medical specialists, psychologists or lawyers. They may need advice in relation to issues of race and culture and assistance from those who have special skills in communications in different languages. They may need advice in relation to those with disabilities, including communication difficulties.

Criteria for Court Orders under Parts IV and V of the Children Act

5.7 The criteria for court orders under Parts IV and V of the Children Act 1989 are based on the concept "significant harm". These criteria for compulsory intervention should always be borne in mind in child protection procedures with careful consideration of the application of the term "significant harm" to the particular case. See Appendix 2 for the complete wording.

(a) For an emergency protection order the court must be satisfied that there is reasonable cause to believe the child is likely to suffer significant harm or the authority is investigating under Section 47 (i.e. reasonable cause to suspect significant harm) and access is frustrated –

(b) For a care or supervision order the likelihood of significant harm must be attributed to the care given to the child or likely to be given to him not being what it would be reasonable to expect a parent to give to him or the child's being beyond parental control.

5.8 The importance of family involvement in child protection work has been increasingly realised and local ACPC procedures must pay full regard to this. Its value lies partly in improving the quality of practice leading to a better outcome for the child and family, and partly in respecting the right of individuals to participate in decisions which concern themselves and their children. At an early stage families and older children should be given information, e.g. by leaflet about child protection procedures.

Records

5.9 The importance of recording at all stages of the child protection process cannot be overemphasised. Evidence from reports, enquiries and reviews into deaths of children indicates the vital importance of good record keeping. Every agency in which staff work with children must have a policy on record keeping and this should include giving all children and parents access to records. Records must be accurate and clear, and contain all the information known to the agency about the child and family. Records need to reflect all the work which is being done by the worker(s) within the agency and they should also indicate working arrangements with staff in other agencies. Good quality records are essential to inform the work at the different stages outlined below and they should contain clear details of the investigation, assessments, the decisions agreed, the basis on which they were made and the plan on which work is based.

STAGES OF WORK IN INDIVIDUAL CASES

5.10 To be effective, co-operation between agencies providing protection to children must be underpinned by a shared agreement about the handling of individual cases. These stages can be identified in the following simple broad terms:

(i) referral and recognition;

(ii) immediate protection and planning the investigation;

(iii) investigation and initial assessment;

(iv) child protection conference and decision making about the need for registration;

(v) comprehensive assessment and planning;

(vi) implementation, review and, where appropriate, de-registration.

These stages do not necessarily stand alone nor are they clearly divided in time. There is likely to be some overlap. The sequence, however, should assist professionals to see more clearly the focus of work at each stage.

5.11 REFERRAL AND RECOGNITION

5.11.1 The starting point of the process is that any person who has knowledge of, or a suspicion that a child is suffering significant harm, or is at risk of significant harm, should refer their concern to one or more of the agencies with statutory duties and/or powers to investigate and intervene – the social services department, the police or the NSPCC. Referrals may come from members of the public, those working with children and families who are not accustomed to dealing with child protection or from other professionals who are regularly engaged in child protection work. All referrals, whatever their origin, must be taken seriously and must be considered with an open mind which does not pre-judge the situation. The statutory agencies must ensure that people know how to refer to them, and they must facilitate the making of referrals and the prompt and appropriate action in response to expressions of concern. It is important in all these cases that the public and professionals are free to refer to the child protection agencies without fear that this will lead to unco-ordinated and/or premature action. The ACPC should publish advice about whom to contact with details of addresses and telephone numbers.

5.11.2 It is essential that professionals who work with children and families should be alert to the signs of child abuse. Locally agreed procedures should make it clear that each agency should provide appropriate training and guidance to ensure that all professionals can recognise signs of abuse and respond appropriately.

5.11.3 The balance needs to be struck between taking action designed to protect the child from abuse whilst at the same time protecting him or her and the family from the harm caused by unnecessary intervention. ACPCs and their constituent agencies should ensure that all staff involved in deciding upon action to be taken following referral have the necessary training, skills and expertise to undertake this complex task. Skills in this area of work are crucial to the immediate and long term safety and well-being of the child.

5.11.4 Except in cases of extreme urgency when immediate protective action is required, referrals will require discussion with other professionals from the child protection agencies and with the referrer. It will be necessary in some cases to seek specialist opinion to enable work to be carried forward.

5.11.5 In some cases courses of action other than a formal investigation will be decided upon following the consultation process. Such a decision should be discussed and agreed by a social worker in consultation with a team leader or supervisor. It is important to keep the referrer and other professionals informed having special regard for confidentiality when the referrer is a member of the public.

5.12 IMMEDIATE PROTECTION AND PLANNING THE INVESTIGATION

5.12.1 Where there is risk to the life of a child or likelihood of serious injury the agencies with the statutory child protection powers need to secure the immediate safety of the child. A decision must be taken urgently as to whether the child should be removed to some other place, either on a voluntary basis or by obtaining an emergency protection order.

5.12.2 If a court order is obtained it will be necessary to plan the work within the timescales set by the court order. If an emergency protection order is granted this gives *authority* to remove the child but the child must not be removed except to safeguard his or her welfare. For instance the order may be obtained on the "frustrated access" criteria but on seeing the child removal may not be indicated. If the child is removed, the applicant must bear in mind the requirement to return the child as soon as it is safe to do so. In some situations it will be possible to ensure the child's safety by the removal of the alleged abuser, or the alleged abuser agreeing to leave the home. The position of any other children in the household must be considered at the same time; the dominant issue must be to ensure the safety of all the children. The urgency of the situation should not detract from every effort being made to ensure that those with parental responsibility are given appropriate opportunity to participate throughout the process, and efforts should be made to facilitate appropriate contact between the family and the child(ren) through the course of the emergency protection order.

5.12.3 Responsibility to ensure that such immediate action is taken rests with the authority where the child is found following the incident. If the child is looked after by another authority or is on the child protection register of another area, the authority taking immediate action should seek, whenever possible, to involve the authority responsible for the child. Only then, if that authority is prepared to accept responsibility, is the first authority absolved from the responsibility to take action. ACPCs should ensure that these points are clear in their procedures.

5.13 Strategy Discussion

5.13.1 It is essential that there is an early *strategy discussion*, which may not require a meeting, between the statutory agencies, i.e. Police and social services, to plan the investigation and in particular the role of each agency and the extent of joint investigation. It is the responsibility of the agency receiving the referral to initiate this. Other team members should be involved as soon as possible. Throughout the first stages of the investigation it is essential for the main agencies to remember that either or both of the civil court child protection and criminal prosecution procedures may be required.

5.13.2 Where the police are undertaking a parallel investigation which may lead to prosecution of an alleged abuser, there are important issues to be considered about the need for the child to receive appropriate counselling and support and the need for the child to appear as a credible witness in court. These questions must be carefully examined in relation to each child in the light of his or her individual needs and the welfare of the child must be of first importance. The advice of specialist professionals such as psychiatrists and psychologists may be useful in reaching a decision, as may discussion by the police with the Crown Prosecution Service.

5.14 INVESTIGATION AND INITIAL ASSESSMENT

5.14.1 There is a duty to investigate whenever the SSD has reason to suspect a child is suffering or is likely to suffer significant harm.

5.14.2 It is essential that local authorities do not lose sight of the need to invoke child protection procedures when a referral or a report is received indicating abuse of a child in a local authority placement. All referrals and allegations from whatever source should be dealt with under the child protection procedures. Whilst acknowledging that there may be matters of disciplinary action or management organisation to pursue separately, the primacy of child protection should be recognised. Issues specific to abuse in various settings, such as foster homes or residential homes, are considered later.

5.14.3 All investigations under Section 47 of the Children Act should take place in accordance with the Area Child Protection Committee procedures. All investigations need to be planned. The prime tasks are:

- to establish the facts about the circumstances giving rise to the concern;
- to decide if there are grounds for concern;
- to identify sources and level of risk; and
- to decide protective or other action in relation to the child and any others.

Sometimes as information emerges during the investigation it will be necessary to take protective action without waiting for the initial child protection conference.

5.14.4 These cases involve both child care and law enforcement issues. What is discovered may be relevant to decisions which have to be taken by both social services and police. Those engaged in planning the investigation will need to involve others with specialist knowledge or particular knowledge of the family as the situation demands. This is not the same as or a substitute for a child protection conference.

Child Assessment Orders

5.14.5 If the investigation is frustrated by the parents but an emergency situation is not identified, an application for a child assessment order (CAO) could be considered. One of the essential ingredients for a child assessment order is that an assessment is needed to help establish basic facts about the child's condition. An application for a child assessment order by a local authority should always be preceded by an investigation under Section 47. Since the application is only to cover non-emergency situations, there will be no justification for the investigation to be merely superficial. The court considering an application will expect to be given details of the investigation and how it arose, including in particular details of the applicant's attempts to be satisfied as to the welfare of the child by arrangements with the people caring for the child. If the court is not satisfied that all reasonable efforts were made to persuade those caring for the child to co-operate and that these efforts were resisted, the application is likely to founder on the grounds that Section 43(1)(c) is not satisfied. For a fuller explanation of this subject, see *Volume 1 – Court Orders* in the Children Act 1989 Guidance and Regulations series. The court will need to be advised about what the assessment should cover in full detail including timing and the need (if this is so) for the child to be kept away from home, and may make directions accordingly. It is important to realise that a child of sufficient understanding to make an informed decision may refuse to consent to the assessment. The order lasts for a maximum of seven days from a named date and the assessment during that period should be designed to secure enough information to decide what further action if any is necessary.

Selection of Staff for Interviewing

5.14.6 During a child protection investigation the child and those personally and professionally connected with the child must be interviewed. Staff should not be selected for this work unless they are of acknowledged competence and have undergone appropriate staff development and training. Those involved in investigations should conduct them under ACPC procedures which should emphasise the need for continual vigilance about the importance of minimising the number of investigative interviews or examinations of the child undertaken. If the investigation is part of the assessment in the course of court proceedings it should be borne in mind that under Rules of Court the court's agreement should be sought for examinations for the purposes of expert evidence. Otherwise the evidence cannot be used unless the court agrees. Workers should begin the investigation process with an open mind to establish whether or not abuse had taken place. Interviewers should retain an open mind so that they can respond to facts as they emerge.

5.14.7 Awareness of the needs of the child should focus the enquiry on the child. Every effort should be made to help him or her to relax and feel at ease. Consideration should be given to the child having a parent, relative, friend or supporter present during the investigative interviews, as the circumstances of the case determine. In spite of these efforts many children and young people will find it difficult to talk about very private matters. They may be reluctant to make statements and accusations the outcome of which they are unsure. The interviewer must listen carefully to what the child has to say and communication with him or her must be in a responsive and receptive manner. He or she must work at the child's pace and use language that the child can understand and thus enable the child to talk about and give as clear an account as possible of events that have taken place. The interviewer must always be open to the possibility that the events have not taken place. Sometimes consideration should be given to the need to provide a separate worker specifically for the parent.

Children and Parents with Communication Difficulties

5.14.8 If the child or parent has communication difficulties, arrangements must be made to help them during interviews. Children with disabilities have the same rights as other children and every effort should be made to provide appropriate assistance during the interview so that they can express themselves fully and so that they can understand what is happening and what decisions have to be made. A sign language interpreter, large print, tape or braille may be needed if communication is to be effective. Children and parents whose first language is not English will also have special needs during the interviews. Efforts should be made to help them have a clear understanding of what is happening and what may happen in the future. Enlisting the services of an interpreter should be considered, but care taken in their choice. Those conducting the investigative interviews with parents and children should be aware of the impact of the interview on longer term plans to help the child as well as the immediate purposes of the interview.

Recording of Interviews

5.14.9 Recording of such interviews should be accurate and should differentiate between fact, hearsay and opinion. Accurate recording will play an important part in future planning and may need to be used in future court action. Care must be taken when audio or video technology is used for recording, especially if the recording may be used in court. In the light of the Children (Admissibility of Hearsay Evidence) Order 1991 (S.I. 1991/1115), there is no restriction under the hearsay rule on the admissibility of videos in family proceedings. New provisions under the Criminal Justice Act 1991 will allow a video recording of an interview with a child to be used as a child's main evidence in criminal proceedings subject to certain conditions. The Home Office is preparing a Code of Practice on the use and storage of video recordings in criminal proceedings and this will cover technical issues as well as child welfare and legal issues. Local ACPC procedures should address the use of video recording in readiness for the implementation of the Criminal Justice Act in 1992, and should draw on the forthcoming Code of Practice.

Where No Substance is Revealed to the Cause for Concern

5.14.10 In circumstances where the investigation reveals no substance to the cause for concern those with parental responsibility, the child (having regard to age, understanding and levels of maturity) and the referrer, as appropriate, should be informed in writing. The process of investigation is painful and difficult for those who undergo it. The fact that the allegation is unsubstantiated may not of itself be a relief. Letters following unsubstantiated allegations should acknowledge this and the distress which has been caused. Consideration should be given to the need for counselling for children and parents involved in the investigation, and a suitably worded apology offered. Attention should be drawn to the duty the statutory agencies have to investigate without leaving investigators open to challenge. It is possible in these situations that services may be required outside the child protection procedures and provision of these should not be precluded as a consequence of the investigation ceasing. It may be difficult for those who have been investigated to accept the services provided by the statutory agency; in these circumstances the agencies should offer advice on alternative sources of support.

5.15 CHILD PROTECTION CONFERENCE AND DECISION MAKING

5.15.1 The child protection conference is an essential stage in joint work in individual cases. In recognition of its central importance, Part 6 looks in detail at the function, organisation and process of the child protection conference. It should be stressed, however, that although central, a child protection conference is only part of the process and should not be a cause for delay in work.

5.15.2 The child protection conference provides the prime forum for professionals and the family to share information and concerns, analyse and weigh up the level of risks to the children and make recommendations for action. It is *not* a forum for a formal decision that a person has abused a child which is a criminal offence. This is a matter for the courts. When a conference concludes that a child's name should be placed on the child protection register, one of the child care agencies with statutory powers (the social services department or the NSPCC) should carry future child care responsibility for the case and designate a member of its social work staff to be the key worker. Each child placed on the child protection register must have a named key worker.

Timing

5.15.3 The time between referral and the initial child protection conference will vary according to the needs of each individual case. The pace should not slacken once the protection of the child is ensured but sufficient time should be taken so that the conference does not result in premature or disorganised action. Initial conferences should take place within eight working days of referral unless there are special reasons why information from the investigation which will lead to a better decision is not available. Normally a maximum of 15 days should be set. If court action is underway the timing of the conference will be determined by the Court Rules.

5.15.4 The only *decision* to be taken at the conference is whether or not to register the child and, if registration is agreed, to allocate the key worker. The key worker must be a social worker, from either the social services department or the NSPCC. When a child is not registered there may still be a need for services. Provision of services should not be dependent on registration.

5.16 COMPREHENSIVE ASSESSMENT AND PLANNING

5.16.1 On registration of a child, the initial plan should include a comprehensive assessment. Its purpose is to acquire a full understanding of the child and family situation in order to provide a sound basis for decisions about future actions. The assessment has to be planned and structured and decisions have to be made in respect of each of the following questions:

- who will undertake the assessment?
- where will it be undertaken?

- what is the timescale?
- how should it be recorded?
- how to involve the family?
- what is the legal status of the child?
- how will it fit in with any court action, and have the necessary steps in relation to this been taken?
- how will it fit with other action, e.g. by the Police in respect of the offence?
- what is the SSD's position regarding parental responsibility?

5.16.2 Such an assessment should include contributions from all relevant agencies to cover social, environmental, medical and developmental circumstances. Some of the families and children will be well known to the child protection agencies and it will be essential to draw on this information and utilise records to the full. Guidance on an approach to assessment can be found in *Protecting Children – A Guide for Social Workers Undertaking a Comprehensive Assessment.*

5.16.3 The comprehensive assessment will inform the child protection plan. It will be the major tool for future work with the child and his or her family who should be encouraged and enabled to participate in the assessment and planning. Although for convenience and clarity comprehensive assessment is described here as a single step, it must be remembered that assessment and re-assessment are continuing activities throughout the child care process.

5.17 NEED FOR A WRITTEN PLAN

5.17.1 A written plan will need to be constructed with the involvement of the carers/parents and in the light of each agency's statutory duties and will identify the contributions each will make the child, to the other family members and the abuser. It will make clear the part to be played by parents, what expectations they may have of agencies and what expectations agencies may have of them. This is separate from the plans required under the Arrangements for Placements Regulations but will need to be consistent with them.

5.17.2 Once the plan has been agreed, it will be the responsibility of individual agencies to implement the parts of the plan relating to them and to communicate with the key worker and others as necessary. The key worker will have the responsibility for pulling together and co-ordinating the contributions of different agencies.

5.17.3 The production of the protection plan must include consideration of the wishes of the child and parents, local resources, the suitability of specialist facilities, their availability for addressing the particular needs of the child and his or her family. Special attention will need to be given to ensuring the services provided under the plan are co-ordinated, structured and ethically and culturally appropriate for the child and the family, with built-in mechanisms for programme review and crisis management.

5.17.4 Children and parents should be given clear information about the purposes and nature of any intervention together with a copy of the plan. Every effort should be made to ensure that they have a clear understanding of the objectives of the plan, that they accept it and are willing to work to it. If the families' preferences about how the work to protect the child should be conducted are not accepted, the reasons for this should be explained, as should their right to complain and make representations.

If the Abuser Goes to Prison

5.17.5 The child protection plan may change significantly if the abuser goes to prison. The plan should recognise that the abuser may want to return home after prison and it should make a statement about what will happen in this event.

5.18.1 In all cases, the inter-agency child protection plan requires regular review to ensure that it continues to provide protection to the child from abuse, that his or her needs are being met and continuing safety is being achieved. Child protection reviews are dealt with in more detail in Part 6. It is recommended that the minimum interval between reviews should be six months, and in addition the social services (and the NSPCC) may convene additional child protection reviews at the request of other professionals as the development of the case requires. For children being looked after, agencies may combine a child protection review under the ACPC child protection procedures with a statutory review of the child. There may well be economies and convenience as a result of combining reviews. It is essential that if the two kinds of review are combined the functions and tasks of each are recognised.

5.18.2 In the case of any child looked after by the local authority (see chapter 2 of Volume 3 of the Children Act Guidance and Regulations), any meeting which is convened for the purpose of considering the child's case in connection with any aspect of the review of that case falls within the Review of Children's Cases Regulations (S.I.1991 no 895). The purpose for which the meeting is convened determines whether it falls under the Regulations, not what the meeting is called.

5.18.3 A review under the Regulations is not a consideration after a complaint or a part of line management supervision of a decision, although either could indicate the need for a review of the child's circumstances.

5.18.4 The decision to remove a child's name from the child protection register can usually only be made at a child protection review (see Part 6). The appropriateness of continuing registration should be considered at every review conference. Parents and child should be fully involved in the decision to remove a child's name from the register. The decision to de-register a child does not mean that there may not be a continuing need for services for the child and the family.

5.19 CHILDREN LIVING AWAY FROM HOME

5.19.1 Children in accommodation provided for them as a service are entitled to the same level and standard of protection from harm as is provided for children in their own homes. ACPC procedures should include a clear policy statement that their agreed local arrangements for the handling of child abuse cases apply in every situation where an allegation of abuse is received in respect of such a child. Individual agencies will need to have clear and unambiguous procedures in line with the ACPC's arrangements. It must be clear that whether the child is placed with a foster parent or living in a residential home or a school, the agencies' actions must take place within the agreed child protection procedures even though other procedures, such as an agency's internal disciplinary procedures or wider considerations about the future of an establishment may need to be pursued in parallel.

CHILDREN IN FOSTER CARE

5.19.2 All agencies need to understand that SSDs have responsibilities for children placed by or on behalf of them with foster parents. In arranging or providing placements with foster parents, the welfare of the child must be safeguarded and promoted. In arranging or supervising these placements, they are required to seek out and pay regard to the wishes and feelings of the child and those of his or her parents. Regulation 7 of the Foster Placement (Children) Regulations requires a local authority to terminate unsatisfactory foster care placements and in some circumstances to remove the child forthwith. This latter eventuality could result from an investigation under Section 47 into the foster child's welfare or of any other child in the foster parent's household. It is important to understand that the SSD's duty to investigate under Section 47, in line with established ACPC procedures, applies equally to children in foster care as it does to children living with their own families. Action taken to investigate allegations of abuse of foster children should also include consideration of the safety of any other children living in the household, including the foster parent's own children.

5.19.3 It is important, too, that all agencies know that where a child not looked after by the SSD is placed by a voluntary organisation with a foster parent, the SSD has duties under Section 62 and the Foster Placement (Children) Regulations 1991 to ensure that the placement safeguards and promotes the welfare of the child by visiting the placement to check that the arrangements are satisfactory. Where the SSD considers that the arrangements are not satisfactory, it is required to arrange for alternative care for the child. Similarly, the SSD's duty to investigate under Section 47 applies equally to these children.

5.19.4 The voluntary organisation's duties to the child contained in section 61 of the Act and the Regulations mentioned above are similar in all respects to those of the SSD. Voluntary organisations should be involved with their local ACPCs to ensure that they participate in agreeing inter-agency child protection procedures. The voluntary organisation's operational procedures should reflect the agreed arrangements and provide clear instructions on how allegations of abuse of a child should be handled.

5.20 CHILDREN IN RESIDENTIAL SETTINGS

5.20.1 All those involved with the provision of care for children in residential settings, including schools, must be alert to the possibility of abuse by other children, visitors and members of staff. Policies and managerial procedures must openly recognise the possibility of abuse and must prevent creating circumstances which could encourage abuse. There must be clear written procedures on how suspected abuse is dealt with, for children and staff to consult and available for external scrutiny.

5.20.2 When abuse occurs within a home or school considerations additional to standard child protection procedures will arise. When abuse is caused by another child resident in the home or school, it is necessary to apply child protection procedures to both the abuser(s) and the victim(s). When the authority looking after both abuser(s) and victim(s) is also the investigating authority, consideration should be given to an independent element being included in the investigation.

Abuse by Visitors

5.20.3 The possibility of abuse by visitors needs to be recognised in the practices related to vetting and recording in the way described in paragraphs 1.179ff of Volume 4 of the Guidance to the Children Act. If such abuse occurs it should normally be dealt with in the same way as stranger abuse.

Abuse by Staff

5.20.4 In order for the abuse by staff to be prevented or readily discovered, it is essential that children and staff are encouraged to report their concerns to the appropriate persons in the local area. The procedure for doing this should be included in the responsible authority's or school's written guidance, and the message reinforced wherever possible through training and supervision. Both children and junior staff will require reassurance about the importance of their making such reports. Those in authority should equally be encouraged to treat all such concerns raised with them by children and junior staff speedily and appropriately, and to ensure that correct and effective action is taken. The procedures should also make clear the action that should be taken if the member of staff feels that inappropriate or insufficient action has been taken.

5.20.5 Where abuse by a member of staff is suspected, the action to be taken would be the same as with any other suspected abuse, i.e. the local SSD or investigating agency should be informed immediately, and other agencies involved as appropriate. In such circumstances the need for the fullest possible co-operation with those investigating the allegations is of great importance, and those with responsibility for the home or school should ensure that this is provided wherever possible.

5.20.6 Investigations of allegations or of suspicions of abuse by a member of the SSD's own staff should, as far as possible, include an independent element. This could, for example, be a representative from another SSD or the local NSPCC. Wherever possible, the investigation of the allegations or suspicions should also be carried out by a senior member of the social services department who does not have immediate line management responsibilities for the home in which the alleged incident has occurred.

5.20.7 It must also be recognised that there may be abuse by staff in a residential setting which pervades the whole staffing fabric with the involvement and collusion of several, possibly senior, members of staff. Where such abuse is suspected, it will be necessary for the police and senior staff from the SSD, when agreeing their strategy for investigation, to pay regard to the need for secrecy, even if this means a delay before action is taken. This will need to be weighed carefully against the rights of the individual children concerned to protection from the suspected abuse.

Opportunities for Outside Contact for Children

5.20.8 Children in residential settings, particularly those with disabilities, may become isolated and have very little opportunity to communicate with people outside of the home or school. This renders such children particularly vulnerable to abuse. Good childcare practice should of course militate against such isolation, but even in the best settings some children find it very difficult to make their problems known. Easy access to a telephone where they can speak privately and publicity about telephone helplines should be available to all children resident in homes and schools. Approved visitors outside of the home should be available to see children who might not feel able to share their problems with staff or their parents.

5.20.9 The need to ensure the safety of children in residential settings including those not looked after by local authorities is recognised in the Act in those sections which require local authorities to visit children in various residential settings, including schools and in the duty of proprietors to safeguard and promote the welfare of the child.

5.20.10 Section 87 of the Children Act gives SSDs the role of inspecting independent boarding schools to help them determine whether a child's welfare is adequately safeguarded and promoted while he is accommodated at the school. During their inspections SSDs will be expected to ensure that the school has in place child protection procedures which comply with this guide and with local ACPCs procedures.

Strands of Investigation

5.20.11 It is important to emphasise, and for all agencies to understand, that in such situations, the guidance provided in paragraphs 1.888–1.889 of Volume 4 of the Children Act series, relating to the three separate strands of investigation to be followed, has particular relevance:

(a) First, there is the child protection investigation, which will be undertaken in accordance with the procedures then in place for dealing with such matters, including a child protection conference, and decisions taken on the action necessary to ensure the continued protection of the child concerned.

(b) Secondly, the circumstances may require a police investigation of whether a crime has been committed.

(c) Thirdly, the employer's disciplinary procedures should be invoked to ascertain whether there has been misconduct or gross misconduct on the part of the staff member.

5.20.12 It is of the greatest importance that those in authority are clear that, although there may be insufficient evidence to support a police prosecution, this does not mean that action does not need to be taken to protect the child, or that disciplinary procedures should not be invoked and pursued.

5.21 NOTIFICATION OF SERIOUS OCCURRENCES

5.21.1 The Foster Placement Regulations require foster parents to agree to notify the SSD or voluntary organisation of any serious illness or occurrence (including disclosure of abuse or an accident) affecting the child (paragraph 8 of Schedule 2). When the SSD or voluntary organisation visits the child, they are required to ensure that a written report is prepared by the person who made the visit (Regulation 6). The Arrangements for Placement Regulations require the child's case record to include copies of any written report about the child and of any document considered or record established in the course of or as a result of a review (Regulation 8). Professionals in all agencies involved with the child should accept that the child protection procedure provides the right mechanism for dealing with such matters.

5.21.2 The Children's Homes Regulations require the responsible authorities for community homes, voluntary homes and registered children's homes (which include certain small independent schools) to provide notifications to specified persons of, amongst other things, serious accidents which include child abuse. The effect of this regulation is to require that the local authority social services department, within whose area the home or school is located, to be informed. When such notifications apply to child abuse the area child protection procedures are the right mechanisms to be applied.

5.22 EXTRA-FAMILIAL ABUSE

5.22.1 Where abuse is carried out by someone other than an adult living in the immediate family, the impact of the abuse on the child and the family is likely to vary according to the nature of the relationship between the child and the abuser, and the nature of the abuse will also be relevant. All such extra-familial abuse should be referred in the same way as intra-familial abuse and receive the same consideration. It is therefore important that inter-agency procedures reflect this requirement.

5.22.2 The processes of recognition, investigation, assessment and planning in cases of abuse carried out by a person who, though not an adult family member, is known to the child and family, are likely to have many of the features found in cases of intra-familial adult/child abuse. Some abuses will be carried out by a person outside of the child's immediate family but known to the child. Such a person may be a member of the extended family, a family friend or acquaintance, or a person who because of professional or voluntary activity has reason to be in contact with a child. Consideration will need to be given to the protection of other children who may continue to have contact with the alleged abuser.

5.23 ABUSE BY A STRANGER OF A CHILD LIVING AT HOME

5.23.1 There are cases in which it is thought that abuse has been carried out by an adult previously unknown to the child and the family. In such cases the application of inter-agency procedures may not be necessary or appropriate for the purpose of investigation but a lack of adequate parental care might be a factor or the child's parents may not be able to give him or her the necessary care, support and protection in the future. The alleged abuser may live with or in close proximity to other children. For all these reasons the police should, at the appropriate time, consult with the social services department to enable them to decide the most suitable course of action. This process should not inhibit the police action to secure evidence on which to prosecute the alleged abuser.

5.23.2 In some cases a decision will be made to hold a child protection conference in respect of the child or any other child who may be considered to be at risk. If a decision is made not to hold a conference, it is important that the parents and the child should be advised of the range of services that statutory and voluntary agencies are able to offer – for example, counselling for the parents and child, therapy for the child. Where available they should be given details of whom to contact to make use of these resources.

5.24 ABUSE CARRIED OUT BY CHILDREN OR YOUNG PEOPLE

5.24.1 When abuse of a child is alleged to have been carried out by another child or young person, it is important that the appropriate child protection procedures should be followed in respect of both the victim and the alleged abuser.

5.24.2 Work with adult abusers has shown that many of them begin committing their abusing acts during childhood or adolescence, and further has indicated that significant numbers have suffered from abusing acts themselves. It is therefore an important child protection function to ensure that such behaviour is treated seriously and is always subject to a referral to child protection agencies. Such adolescent abusers are themselves in need of services.

5.24.3 Upon receipt of such referral there should be a child protection conference in respect of the alleged abuser to address current knowledge of:

- the alleged abuser
- their family circumstances
- the offence committed
- the level of understanding he or she has of the offence
- the need for further work.

This should include consideration of possible arrangements for accommodation, education (where applicable) and supervision in the short term pending the compilation of a comprehensive assessment. This assessment should ideally involve a child psychiatrist to look at issues of risk and treatment.

5.24.4 Membership and handling of the conference, including initial plans, should be as prescribed in the standard child protection conference.

5.24.5 The conference should re-convene following the completion of the comprehensive assessment, to review the plan in light of the information obtained and to co-ordinate the interventions designed to dissuade the abuser from committing further abusive acts. Experience suggests that in many cases, policies of minimal intervention are not as effective as focussed forms of therapeutic intervention which may be under orders of the civil or criminal courts.

5.25 WORK WITH ADULT ABUSERS

5.25.1 The first task of the child protection agencies is the immediate protection of the child but increasingly the need to work with adult abusers is being recognised as an important preventative function, and there is a growing understanding that the mere removal of abusers from the vicinity of their present victims is too simplistic a solution to a complex problem. All the child protection agencies have some contact with abusers; some, such as social services departments and probation, have more specific roles in working with abusers and their families. ACPCs should include work with abusers in their procedures and annual reports.

5.26 ORGANISED ABUSE

Definition

5.26.1 For the purposes of this Guide organised abuse is a generic term which covers abuse which may involve a number of abusers, a number of abused children and young people and often encompass different forms of abuse. It involves, to a greater or lesser extent, an element of organisation.

5.26.2 A wide range of abusing activity is covered by this term, from small paedophile or pornographic rings, often but not always organised for profit, with most participants knowing one another, to large networks of individual groups or families which may be spread more widely and in which not all participants will be known to each other. Some organised groups may use bizarre or ritualised behaviour, sometimes associated with particular "belief" systems. This can be a powerful mechanism to frighten the abused children into not telling of their experiences. Research suggests some caution in sharp distinctions between types of abuser. Most child sexual abusers share characteristics which suggest a calculated recidivist pattern of activity, where multiple abuse acts and possibly multiple victims are involved. "Paedophiles" may also abuse within their own homes and "incest" offenders may abuse children outside the family.

5.26.3 Knowledge is growing in this area of abuse and the Department of Health has commissioned research into its frequency and characteristics. Some authorities have had experience in this complex area of work and have lessons to share with those who have yet to experience this phenomenon.

Need for ACPC Procedure

5.26.4 Investigations which come within the category of organised abuse will put inter-agency procedures to the test. It is essential that such investigations are managed at an appropriate senior level and conducted by staff trained and experienced in joint child abuse investigations. Appropriate procedures, which build upon the principles of *Working Together*, should be agreed through the ACPC for dealing with organised abuse. Individual agencies will need to consider implications for practice. The single most important consideration is the safety and well-being of the child.

Timing of Intervention

5.26.5 As in other forms of abuse described in this document, decisions about the form and timing of the investigation should be agreed at a strategy discussion involving staff from the main child protection agencies. Any adjustment to the plan for action should be reviewed if necessary by this group. The first priority should always be the need to protect children, but the knowledge that in cases of organised abuse the risk to children will escalate if abusers avoid detection must be considered. This will mean that on occasion those professionals involved will need to weigh the risk of delaying an investigation and the implications this has for individual child(ren) against the benefits of the collection of evidence against an abuser or group of abusers, and the consequent benefit to a wider group of children if the case is conclusive.

5.26.6 There may be pressures to intervene more speedily in those cases which could lead to children being removed from home too quickly. The removal of children from their homes can cause great distress to the child and be very damaging for the rest of the family. Except where the child is in acute physical danger, the timing of the removal of children from their homes should be agreed following consultation with all appropriate professionals, the welfare of the individual child(ren) being the first consideration.

5.26.7 Care must be taken in large scale investigations to ensure that staff do not concentrate on the legal aspects of the investigation at the expense of the welfare issues. It is recognised that the standard of evidence for criminal proceedings differs from that required for child protection purposes. This should be acknowledged in the ACPC procedures and emphasis given to the protection of the child as a prime consideration.

Involvement of Senior Managers

5.26.8 It is important that senior managers from the investigating agencies are informed as soon as suspicions relating to the existence of organised abuse begin to emerge, so that proper consideration can be given as to how an inter-agency investigation should be conducted ensuring supervision at an appropriate level in accordance with agreed procedures. Investigations of this nature are likely to bring considerable media and public attention; there is benefit, therefore, in there being agreed procedures between the police and social services in relation to dealings with the media. Media management is also a matter which should be covered in ACPC procedures.

5.26.9 There will be occasions when the child's need for immediate therapy overrides the need for the child to appear as a credible witness in a criminal case. This needs to be weighed up and a decision made on the basis of the available knowledge. There should always be discussions with the Crown Prosecution Service on the particular needs of the child, and the needs of the child are of prime importance. The agencies should co-operate in assessing what is required and pool their resources to meet the diverse needs of individual children.

Resource Considerations

5.26.10 There are considerable resource implications in the handling of organised abuse. Senior managers need to address such issues from the standpoint of their own agency and in discussion with managers from other agencies with whom they collaborate. It is important to begin planning the handling of organised abuse as soon as possible and it is necessary to address a number of questions, for example:

(a) Is there sufficient accommodation for interviewing?

(b) Are there sufficient facilities for recording?

(c) Are there sufficient interviewers?

(d) Are there enough foster parents and residential workers appropriately prepared to support the children?

(e) Are there appropriate support and supervision systems for staff?

Need for Co-operation across Geographic Boundaries

5.26.11 Organised abuse does not recognise the conventions of geographic boundaries and it will be necessary for ACPCs to consider establishing links with neighbouring authorities to ensure consistency of approach. Such links may also provide for a pooling of resources, e.g. skilled staff and specialist resources, such as video studios, in the event of such an occurrence.

Need for Regular Strategy Meetings

5.26.12 Arrangements should be made for regular multi-agency strategy meetings when organised abuse is being handled. The aim should be to review activity frequently to ensure that it complies with agreed child protection practice and procedures and continues to engage the active co-operation of all agencies.

5.26.13 Much attention is focussed on the investigation of organised abuse. However, as with other forms of abuse the investigation is only the beginning of the process, and once this has been completed there will be treatment work to be done with the children and their families. The same considerations about the need for and nature of therapeutic help or intervention apply in these cases, as in any other case.

PART 6

THE CHILD PROTECTION CONFERENCE AND THE CHILD PROTECTION REGISTER

CHILD PROTECTION CONFERENCES

6.1 The child protection conference is central to child protection procedures. It is *not* a forum for a formal decision that a person has abused a chld. That is a matter for the courts. It brings together the family and the professionals concerned with child protection and provides them with the opportunity to exchange information and plan together. The conference symbolises the inter-agency nature of assessment, treatment and the management of child protection. Throughout the child protection process, the work is conducted on an inter-agency basis and the conference is the prime forum for sharing information and concerns, analysing risk and recommending responsibility for action. It draws together the staff from all the agencies with specific responsibilities in the child protection process (health, social services, police, schools and probation), and other staff who can offer relevant specialist advice, for example psychiatrists, psychologists, lawyers, and provides them with the forum for conducting and agreeing their joint approach to work with the child and family.

6.2 There are two kinds of child protection conference:

* the initial child protection conference
  and
* the child protection review.

The use of these terms is recommended to ensure clarity and to distinguish the meetings organised under the ACPC procedures from other case discussions. These should be kept to a minimum while a child protection case is being handled to avoid confusion, although separate discussions between the major agencies to review the strategy of the investigation may be needed. The child protection conference should have distinct and clearly defined functions and tasks. The ACPC procedures should detail these functions and should address issues of membership and process in relation to both initial child protection conference and child protection reviews.

The Responsibility to Convene a Child Protection Conference

6.3 A child protection conference will be convened by the agency with statutory powers (the SSD or the NSPCC) following an investigation and indication that a decision has to be made about further action under the child protection procedures. At the time of the initial conference, it will be agreed if and when a child protection review will be needed. In addition, any concerned professional may ask the agency with statutory powers to convene a child protection review when he or she believes that the child is not adequately protected or when there is a need for a change to the child protection plan. If a child's name is placed on the child protection register, a review conference should be held at a time agreed at the initial conference and the intervening period should be no more than six months. For the first review it will be less, unless the initial conference had before it enough material to assess fully the risk to the child.

Purpose of the Initial Child Protection Conference

6.4 An initial child protection conference should be called only after an investigation under Section 47 of the Children Act has been made into the incident or suspicion of abuse which has been referred. The timing of the initial conference is dealt with in Part 5, and it is emphasised that it should not be convened until relevant information and reports are available to inform the decisions of the conference. All initial conferences should normally take place within eight working days of referral except where there are particular reasons for delay such as the need to get far enough with the assessment to plan for the future needs of the child, provided the court process does not entail an earlier date.

6.5 The initial child protection conference brings together family members and professionals from the agencies which are concerned with child care and child protection to share and evaluate the information gathered during the investigation, to make decisions about the level of risk to the child(ren), to decide on the need for registration and to make plans for the future. If a decision to register is made, it will be necessary to appoint a named key worker and make recommendations for a core group of professionals to carry out the inter-agency work.

6.6 It is not appropriate for anyone other than a social worker from either the SSD or the NSPCC to be a key worker. This does not mean that he or she will be the person with the most face-to-face contact with the family or play the most active role in treatment or service delivery. The key worker's role derives from the role of the lead agency, that is the agency with statutory powers.

6.7 The key worker has two main tasks. He or she must fulfil the statutory responsibilities of his or her agency which will include the development of a multi-agency, multi-disciplinary plan for the protection of the child. The key worker also has a responsibility to act as lead worker for the inter-agency work in this case. In this role he or she will provide a focus for communication between professionals involved and will co-ordinate the inter-agency contributions to the assessment, planning and review of this case. The key worker must also ensure that parents and children are fully engaged in the implementation of the child protection plan.

6.8 The only decision for an initial child protection conference is whether or not to register the child. It discusses and records a proposed plan of action and it is for each agency representative to decide whether to accept the recommendations for action and their part in the plan. There should be a locally agreed procedure for confirming that these recommendations will be acted upon. It is essential that parents, and children where appropriate, should be fully involved in the discussions about what should constitute a plan. Agreement should be striven for between the professionals, the family and the child. Making a formal agreement is in itself a useful way to record plans. Authorities may find it helpful to consider the Family Rights Group model agreement.

Purpose of the Child Protection Review

6.9 The child protection review has been mentioned in Part 5. The purpose is to review the arrangements for the protection of the child, examine the current level of risk and ensure that he or she continues to be adequately protected, consider whether the inter-agency co-ordination is functioning effectively and to review the protection plan. Every child protection review should consider whether registration should be continued or ended. The first review conference may be the occasion for the production of the full child protection plan, based on the comprehensive assessment.

The Organisation of the Child Protection Conference

6.10 Child protection conferences are only fully effective and useful if they have a clearly defined purpose and are task centred, chaired by an experienced and trained person. For reasons of both efficiency and confidentiality, the number of people involved in a conference should be limited to those who need to know and to those who have a contribution to make. In addition there should be proper administrative arrangements for convening conferences and producing minutes. The involvement of parents and children in the child protection process requires that conferences are well organised and managed.

The Involvement of Children, Parents, and Carers
in Child Protection Conferences

6.11 This Guide stresses the need to ensure that the welfare of the child is the overriding factor guiding child protection work. It also emphasises the importance of professionals working in partnership with parents and other family members or carers and the concept of parental responsibility. These principles must underpin all child protection work. The following paragraphs deal with parental and family involvement in child protection conferences. However, it cannot be emphasised too strongly that involvement of children and adults in child protection conferences will not be effective unless they are fully involved from the outset in all stages of the child protection process, and unless from the time of referral there is as much openness and honesty as possible between families and professionals.

Conflict between Parents and between Parents and Children

6.12 It should be recognised that the interests of parents and children may conflict and that in such cases the child's interests should be the priority. It will sometimes be appropriate to work differently with each of the parents, for example, if one is the alleged abuser or if there is a high level of parental conflict.

Involvement of Children

6.13 A local authority has a specific duty to promote the welfare of the child looked after. In relation to any decisions taken, the authority has a duty to ascertain as far as is practicable his or her wishes and feelings and give due consideration to them, having regard to his or her age and understanding. Whenever children have sufficient understanding and are able to express their wishes and feelings and to participate in the process of investigation, assessment, planning and review, they should be encouraged to attend conferences. They may feel more able to do so if there is a friend or supporter present. The advice on arrangements to facilitate attendance of a child and parents at meetings in paragraph 8.16 of Volume 3 of the Children Act guidance is relevant. See also Volume 6 of the same series. If a child does not wish to attend, or his or her age and/or understanding makes this inappropriate, the conference should be provided with a clear and up-to-date account of the child's views by the professionals who are working with the child. The conference should, therefore, expect the key worker to be able to inform them about the views of a child who is not attending the meeting. Equally the professional who is working most closely with a child should keep the child informed about the decisions and recommendations reached at the conference and any changes in the inter-agency protection plan.

6.14 It is important that ACPCs should formally agree the principle of including parents and children in all conferences. Guidance on their inclusion must be contained in the local child protection procedures.

Exclusion from Child Protection Conferences

6.15 While there may be exceptional occasions when it will not be right to invite one or other parent to attend a case conference in whole or in part, exclusion should be kept to a minimum and needs to be especially justified. The procedure should lay down criteria for this, including the evidence required. A strong risk of violence, with supporting evidence, by the parents towards the professionals or the child might be one example or evidence that the conference would be likely to be disrupted. The possibility that one of the parents may be prosecuted for an offence against the child does not in itself justify exclusion.

6.16 The decision to exclude a parent, carer or child from a child protection conference should rest with the chair of the conference who should base his or her decision on the exclusion criteria in the local child protection procedures. The decision to exclude a child and his or her parent or parents, and the reason for doing so, should be recorded on the child's file. Adults who wish to make representations at the conference may not all wish to speak in front of each other. There may also be times when the wish of the child to attend and the wish of the parent to do so are in conflict and there will be a need to make arrangements to accommodate both. These issues can be covered in broad terms in the local child protection procedures but a decision will have to be made by the chair in relation to each individual case.

6.17 If parents are excluded or are unable or unwilling to attend a child protection conference it is important that they are encouraged to find a method of communicating their views to the conference. This may be done by means of a letter or a tape recording, or the social worker and/or another professional may agree with the parent that they should represent the parent's views and wishes.

Involvement of Others

6.18 It may be that the parent or relative will feel more confident to attend if they are encouraged to bring a friend or supporter. If they are accompanied by a friend or professional such as a lawyer, it will be incumbent on the chair to clarify the role of the additional person. The conference is not a tribunal to decide whether abuse has taken place and legal representation is therefore not appropriate.

Minutes

6.19 Following the child protection conference, those present should receive the minutes of that conference. Others who were not present for the whole or part of the conference such as parents and other relevant family members and professionals should receive as a minimum written confirmation of the main findings of the conference, a note of who attended and who was absent and confirmation of the decisions and recommended plan of action (see the requirements in respect of written agreements in regulation of placements. Volume 3 of Children Act Guidance refers). It is important that this summary paper should be prepared and distributed speedily although the production of the full conference minutes may take longer. The summary of the meeting should be discussed with the parents and children as appropriate in order to ensure that they are clear about the expectations professionals have of them and the expectations they have of the professionals.

Removal of Names from Register

6.20 When a child's name is placed on the register the reason for this decision should be made clear to the child (if old enough) and to the parents. It should be explained to them how registration and the child protection plan are linked. They should be advised on the procedure for the removal of the child's name from the register and how and when this could happen. It is important that parents are clear about where the responsibility for decision making lies. For example, the decision to initiate care proceedings lies with the agencies with statutory powers not with the conference.

6.21 Parents who wish to discuss or challenge a decision of this kind need to take it up in the first instance with the agency concerned. It is not a matter for the inter-agency child protection conference. Similarly, families who have a complaint about a particular agency's services should take it up with the agency concerned. All agencies should ensure that they have clear procedures which will enable parents and children to pursue complaints. Local authorities are required by Section 26 of the Children Act to establish complaints procedures, and parents should be provided with information about these procedures. Other agencies will have their own complaints procedures and complaints about a member or chair of a conference should normally be made to the appropriate employing authority. ACPC procedures should cover the handling of complaints about a conference as such. ACPCs could establish a special "appeals procedure", or look to the procedure of the local authority as the lead agency. It is important however not to see the conference as in any sense a quasi legal tribunal from which a right of appeal might be expected.

Decisions Not to Register

6.22 If it is decided at the child protection conference that the investigation is completed and the level of risk does not warrant registration, this should be confirmed with the parents and the child, if appropriate, in writing by the chair of the conference. Written confirmation is important even if the parents were at the conference. Such a letter should acknowledge the inevitable distress caused by an investigation but it should also explain that there is a statutory obligation to investigate allegations. The letter should make clear that even though there has been no registration, the parents are still eligible for services for themselves and their children. Supportive counselling may be appropriate and should be offered. However, the counsellor may have to be a worker who has had no connection with the investigation.

Encouragement of Participation of Children and Family Adults

6.23 There are a variety of practical ways in which the participation of adults in the family and children at conferences can be encouraged and made less difficult. For example, conferences should be held at a time and place which is convenient for the family as well as the professional workers; the family should be prepared for the conference by the professional worker with whom they have the closest relationship; they should meet the chair in advance; the parents and caring adults should be made aware of the issues to be discussed at the conference so that they can seek advice and prepare their point of view; the size of the professional group should be limited to those who really need to attend; and comfortable waiting facilities should be available. It is details such as these that ACPCs will need to address in their local procedures. Some of the advice below about the handling of conferences will also serve to ease the position of families on these occasions and thus encourage their participation.

Attendance at the Child Protection Confernce

6.24 Those who attend conferences should be there because they have a contribution to make. Meetings that are unnecessarily large inhibit discussion and do not use valuable resources to the best advantage. Large numbers of professionals, some of whom make no apparent contribution, are particularly inhibiting to parents and children who will in any event probably find the conference a difficult occasion.

6.25 All the agencies which have specific responsibilities in the child protection process should be invited to send representatives. These include:

- the social services,
- the NSPCC (when operational in the area),
- the police,
- education (when the child is of school age),

- the health authority,
- the general medical practitioner,
- the health visiting service,
- the probation service,
- appropriate voluntary organisations, and
- a representative of the armed services in each case where there is a Service connection.

6.26 All those who are invited should be informed that the child, the parents and other carers have been invited. A child protection conference may be a large gathering in the early stages of work, where a number of agencies may be contributing to an investigation or an assessment for planning. However, once a long term plan has been formulated, and a group led by the key worker has been identified to work with the family, the number attending the child protection review will probably be reduced. It is the responsibility of the chair to ensure that the appropriate people are invited to the conference.

6.27 The chair must be able to call on advice from a lawyer from the local authority's legal section particularly when court action is under consideration and on other specialist advice when necessary, for example, the advice of a psychiatrist, psychologist or workers and interpreters with special knowledge either of working with people with a disability or of working with people from a particular race or culture.

6.28 On occasions it may be useful to invite others working with the family to join in the conference, for example, volunteer workers. It will be necessary for the key worker or the person most closely involved to brief him or her about the purpose of the conference, the duty of confidentiality and the primacy of the child's interest. Issues about attendance, written contributions and substitute representation are matters to be addressed in the local child protection procedures.

Chairing Child Protection Conferences

6.29 Child protection conferences must be chaired by a member of staff from the social services department (or the NSPCC if there is a local arrangement to this effect). The choice will be particularly important if abuse is suspected in an establishment run by or on behalf of the local authority, or in a placement arranged by them. The skills of the chair are crucial to the effectiveness of the inter-agency child protection conference. The chair should have a good understanding and professional knowledge of child protection. The selection and necessary training of those who chair child protection conferences is of great importance.

6.30 The conference chair must ensure that the conference focusses on the child as the primary client whose interests must transcend those of the parents and other carers when there is any conflict. The chair must be able to take an objective view of the case under discussion and line managers, who have been or will be involved in making decisions about the case, should not chair child protection conferences. There are considerable advantages in having the same person to chair all conferences which are held in relation to a specific child.

6.31 The chair has a key role in establishing the ethos at the child protection conference. He or she needs to be clear about the purpose of the meeting, the work to be done, the roles of all the participants including parents, children and the professionals, the waiting arrangements for parents and children who may not be able to remain throughout the conference. The chair should also emphasise the confidential nature of the occasion and of the reports and information shared. The chair should enable all those present to make their full contribution to the discussion.

Administrative Arrangements

6.32 Sound administrative arrangements are essential to support the child protection conference process, and this is a matter which must be addressed in the local child protection procedures. A system should be established which ensures that the appropriate people are invited to each conference and that they are given as much warning as possible of when and where it will be held. It should be held in a place and at a time which ensure the maximum attendance possible, and particularly the attendance of the relevant people working with the family.

Reports for the Child Protection Conference

6.33 There should be an expectation that all those attending a conference will prepare for it. Investigating officers and key workers, in particular, should prepare thoroughly and will normally provide written reports covering both past and present incidents of abuse, information about the family circumstances, details of work undertaken and proposals for the future. Other professional workers should be encouraged to have available at conferences other written reports to which they can refer. For example, school reports, police statements and medical reports including growth charts could be useful. Whilst the clear intention is to make available to the conference information from such written reports the chair must emphasise the confidential nature of this shared information. Authors of reports should take care to distinguish between fact, observation, allegation and opinion. Those unable to attend the conference should communicate their comments in writing to the chair for inclusion in the discussion.

Record of the Conference

6.34 All child protection conferences must have someone whose sole task is to take notes and produce minutes of the meeting. This person must be trained for the task before undertaking it. The conference chair should never take the notes.

6.35 The written record of the child protection conference is a crucial working tool for all professionals. It should detail the essential facts, the decisions and the recommendations, the inter-agency child protection plan and an account of the discussion on which the decisions and recommendations are based. A copy of the minutes should be sent to all those who attended the conference. People receiving the minutes should be required to draw attention to any inaccuracies. The minutes should be despatched as quickly as possible. If the parents or older child did not attend the whole or part of a conference, it may not be appropriate for them to receive the full version, but at the minimum, a summary of decisions and plans should be sent to them. The minutes are confidential and should not be passed to third parties without the consent of the child protection conference chair. Every agency should ensure that there are safe storage arrangements for the minutes. They are essential to the continuing work with the family and should be circulated as soon as possible so that inter-agency work may progress.

CHILD PROTECTION REGISTERS

6.36 In each area covered by a social services department, a central register must be maintained which lists all the children in the area who are considered to be suffering from or likely to suffer significant harm and for whom there is a child protection plan. This is not a register of children who have been abused but of children for whom there are currently unresolved child protection issues and for whom there is an inter-agency protection plan. The registers should include children who are recognised to be at risk and who are placed in the local authority's area by another local authority or agency. Registration does not of itself provide any protection and it must lead to an inter-agency protection plan. Registration should not be used to obtain resources which might otherwise not be available to the family.

The Purpose of the Register

6.37 The purpose of the register is to provide a record of all children in the area for whom there are unresolved child protection issues and who are currently the subject of an inter-agency protection plan and to ensure that the plans are formally reviewed every six months. The register will provide a central point of speedy inquiry for professional staff who are worried about a child and want to know whether the child is the subject of an inter-agency protection plan. The register will also provide useful information for the individual child protection agencies and for the ACPC in its policy development work and strategic planning.

Criteria for Registration

6.38 The inclusion of a child's name on the child protection register will only occur following a child protection conference. The exception is when a child on another register moves into the area. Such children will be registered immediately pending the first child protection conference in the new area.

Requirements for Registration

6.39 Before a child is registered the conference must decide that there is, or is a likelihood of, significant harm leading to the need for a child protection plan. One of the following requirements needs to be satisfied:

(i)   There must be one or more identifiable incidents which can be described as having adversely affected the child. They may be acts of commission or omission. They can be either physical, sexual, emotional or neglectful. It is important to identify a specific occasion or occasions when the incident has occurred. Professional judgement is that further incidents are likely;

or

(ii) Significant harm is expected on the basis of professional judgement of findings of the investigation in this individual case or on research evidence.

The conference will need to establish so far as they can a cause of the harm or likelihood of harm. This cause could also be applied to siblings or other children living in the same household so as to justify registration of them. Such children should be categorised according to the area of concern.

Categories of Abuse for Registration

6.40 The following categories should be used for the register and for statistical purposes. They are intended to provide definitions as a guide for those using the register. In some instances, more than one category of registration may be appropriate. This needs to be dealt with in the protection plan. The statistical returns will allow for this. Multiple abuse registration should not be used just to cover all eventualities.

Neglect: The persistent or severe neglect of a child, or the failure to protect a child from exposure to any kind of danger, including cold or starvation, or extreme failure to carry out important aspects of care, resulting in the significant impairment of the child's health or development, including non-organic failure to thrive.

Physical Injury: Actual or likely physical injury to a child, or failure to prevent physical injury (or suffering) to a child including deliberate poisoning, suffocation and Munchausen's syndrome by proxy.

Sexual Abuse: Actual or likely sexual exploitation of a child or adolescent. The child may be dependent and/or developmentally immature.

Emotional Abuse: Actual or likely severe adverse effect on the emotional and behavioural development of a child caused by persistent or severe emotional ill-treatment or rejection. All abuse involves some emotional ill-treatment. This category should be used where it is the main or sole form of abuse.

6.41 These categories for child protection register purposes do not tie in precisely with the definition of "significant harm" in Section 31 of the Children Act which will be relevant if Court proceedings are initiated. For example, with a case of neglect it will be necessary to consider whether it involves actual or likely "significant harm", and whether it involves "ill treatment" or "impairment of health or development" (in each case as defined by the Act). The Courts may well provide an interpretation of "sexual abuse" (which is not defined in the Act) which is different from that used above in particular cases, in which case their definition should be used in relation to those cases.

Pre-birth Child protection Conferences

6.42 On occasions there will be sufficient concern about the future risk to an unborn child to warrant the implementation of child protection procedures and the calling of a child protection conference to consider the need for registration and the need for a child protection plan. Such a conference should have the same status and be conducted in the same manner as an initial child protection conference. Those who would normally attend an initial child protection conference should be invited. Parents or carers should be invited as to other child protection conferences and should be fully involved in plans for the child's future. If a decision is made that the child's name needs to go on the child protection register, the main cause for concern should determine the category of registration.

Criteria for De-registration

6.43 De-registration should be considered at every child protection review. Additionally any of the agencies involved with the child may request that a conference is convened to consider the possibility of de-registration.

6.44 For de-registration to occur all the members of the review conference must be satisfied that the abuse or risk of abuse (either the original type or any other) is no longer present or is no longer of a level to warrant registration. Their decision must be based on a careful and thorough analysis of current risk.

6.45 Reasons for de-registration can be grouped under headings.

(i) **The original factors which led to registration** no longer apply – this would include:

a child who has remained at home but abuse or the risk of abuse has been reduced by work with the family and through the protection plan;

the child who has been placed away from home and there is no longer access to the abusing adult or the access is no longer considered to present a risk to the child;

where the abusing adult is no longer a member of the same household as the child and there is no contact or such contact as occurs is no longer considered to be a risk to the child;

the completion of the comprehensive assessment and a detailed analysis of risk has shown that registration is no longer required and child protection is not necessary.

(ii) **The child and family have moved permanently to another area** and that area has accepted responsibility for the future management of case.

(iii) **The child is no longer a child in the eyes of the law**

This includes:

- the child who reaches 18 years of age
- the child who gets married.

(iv) **The child dies**.

6.46 The first category of criteria for de-registration always requires a conference. The other categories may be agreed without the need for a meeting.

Removal of Names from Register

6.47 If the child protection conference agrees that the child's name should be removed from the child protection register this must be recorded in the minutes. Dissenting views or failure to agree must be recorded. ACPC procedures will need to address the problem of resolving disagreements about de-registration.

6.48 De-registration should not lead to automatic cessation of services, and the professionals involved should discuss with the parents and the child what services might be needed following de-registration. With a young person approaching the age of 18 it would be good practice to consult with the young person in advance about the inevitable de-registration to establish what help he or she would find useful. The decision of the review and future plans should be confirmed in writing as usual with all those present.

Management of the Register

6.49 It is recommended that the register is established and maintained by the social services department (or the NSPCC on its behalf). The register should be held separately from agency records, in conditions safeguarding confidentiality. It should be managed by an experienced social worker with knowledge and skills in child abuse work (the register "custodian"). Information about how to contact the register should be available to all agencies concerned.

6.50 Some registers are now computerised and this can lead to uncontrolled access to information if appropriate steps are not taken to prevent unauthorised access. This undermines the confidentiality of the register. This and other issues related to computerised registers should be covered in ACPC procedures. A record should be kept of any children not on the register about whom enquiries are made, and of the advice given. If the child's name is on the register when an enquiry is made the name of the key worker should be given to the enquirer. If a child's name is not on the register when an enquiry is made but there is another child on the register at the same address the custodian should see that this is followed up.

6.51 The Department of Health holds a list of custodians of child protection registers for England and Welsh Office for Wales. Whenever a change is made this should be notified to Community Services Division at Wellington House, Waterloo Road, London SE1 8UG or Public Health and Family Division at Welsh Office, Cathays Park, Cardiff as appropriate so that the list can be kept up to date.

Information About Abusers

6.52 Some local authorities and other agencies have found it helpful for general social work and child protection purposes to maintain a list of all offenders in the area who have been convicted of offences listed in Schedule I of the Children and Young Persons Act 1933. Such a list has its limitations because it is difficult to keep it up to date. Although the prison service, through the probation service, notifies local authority social service departments of the discharges of Schedule I, offenders such people are often highly mobile.

6.53 Appendix 4 advises that child protection registers should include information on relevant offences committed by members of and regular visitors to the household. Who constitutes a "regular visitor" will be a matter of judgement in relation to the circumstances of the case and would normally be identified in the course of the comprehensive assessment of the family. A "relevant offence" will be an offence established by a criminal conviction which is relevant to the reasons for which the child is thought to be at risk and the child's name entered on the register. Information about such offences will normally emerge from the assessment of the family or at the initial conference but should also be considered during child protection reviews, particularly if the household composition has changed. It is not envisaged that the names of members of, or regular visitors to the household will be automatically checked against police records except where there are grounds to suspect the individual concerned.

6.54 Care should be taken with case records which contain information about adults suspected but not convicted of offences against children and a list of such people should not be held. The confidentiality of such records must be safeguarded and should not be shared except for child protection purposes. Any publicity given to such records could leave the agency subject to legal challenge. Where there is information about an abuser they must be informed and told of the possibility of questioning the details or making representations about the entry. See R. v Norfolk County Council ex parte M. [1989] 3 WLR 502 and R. v Harrow LBC ex parte D [1989] 3 WLR 1239.

JOINT TRAINING

7.1 Effective child protection depends not only on reliable and accepted systems of co-operation, but also on the skills, knowledge and judgement of all staff working with children in relation to child protection matters. It is important therefore that people in direct contact with children receive training to raise their awareness of the predisposing factors, signs and symptoms and local procedures relating to all child abuse matters. Staff with major roles in child protection will need specific training which will include skills such as recognition of the need to work in partnership with parents and to take full account of the implications of race, culture and any disabilities when assessing a family's situation. Single agency training is outside the scope of this Guide, which focusses on **the Joint Training** needed to complement the action of individual agencies to promote the training and development of their own staff.

JOINT INVESTIGATION

7.2 Specialist training is required for selected staff of social services departments, the NSPCC, the health service and the police who will be involved in the joint investigation of cases and subsequent intervention. Training material is being developed to complement the Home Office Code of Practice on the use of video in interviewing child witnesses in criminal cases. Further developments are expected in production of training on interviewing children more generally. Details can be obtained from the child abuse training unit at the National Children's Bureau, who act as a clearing house for the evaluation of training materials and dissemination of information, funded by the Department of Health.

7.3 Training for the joint interviewing of children is carried out by police services and their corresponding local social services departments. The aim of this training is to enable members of each service to understand one another's role fully, to learn how to work together on a joint interviewing team on cases which may lead to criminal proceedings and, above all, to learn how to interview children who may have been badly abused by other adults in such a way as to encourage them to provide information without further hurting them. Interviews must always and only be conducted in the best interests of the child.

PROFESSIONAL STAFF

7.4 It is recommended that agencies establish joint annual training programmes on child abuse issues with access for all professional groups in direct contact with children and families. These programmes, preferably involving trainers from a variety of relevant agencies, should help staff in each agency understand the respective roles of the other agencies, and thus promote good working relationships. The senior social worker providing expert advice to the local authority should play a central role in the development and monitoring of the arrangements for such training under the auspices of the ACPC. The key task will be to ensure that these training opportunities are available and known to staff in all the relevant agencies. Local authority lawyers who are involved with child care law should also be included in suitable programmes both as trainers and to keep abreast of recent developments in practice.

7.5 The level and type of training to be provided will depend upon the degree of involvement that the staff of particular agencies have in child protection work. All relevant staff should be trained in the recognition of signs of possible abuse and what immediate action to take.

OTHER STAFF

7.6 Telephonists and receptionists employed in the various agencies involved in the provision of services for children should be given clear instructions on what to do if contacted by anyone wishing to report suspected child abuse.

DEVELOPMENT OF TRAINING OPPORTUNITIES

7.7 Education and training are not luxuries; it is essential that all members of staff working in child protection are properly trained for the jobs which they are expected to do. Inter-agency training is essential if inter-agency procedures are to function satisfactorily. Agencies should also make sure that education and training are seen as integral components of all jobs. For social services the new Central Council for Education and Training in Social Work (CCETSW) framework for post qualifying education and training means that training can be part of every social worker's career, whether in practice, research, management or education/training.

7.8 All social service staff who work in child care and child protection services, together with foster parents with whom local authorities have boarded out children and local authority sponsored childminders, are eligible for training under the Training Support Programme. Social services departments are encouraged to support the development of inter-agency and multi-disciplinary training for all staff engaged in child protection work and to provide places on their training courses for staff from the independent sectors.

7.9 The developing CCETSW post qualifying framework (see CCETSWA Paper 31) is much more flexible than the previous provision of a limited number of post qualifying courses in child protection. All social workers will be able to accumulate credits towards two levels of post qualifying training, a post qualifying level and an Advanced Award level. The framework is based on a Credit Accumulation and Transfer System (CATS). Where possible and appropriate, staff should be seconded to these courses. At present CCETSW have 10 consortia developing curricula for post qualifying studies including child protection. Currently the CATS points are only available for social work staff but consortia will be required to ensure that provision is made for joint training. A total of 30 consortia are planned for the UK.

7.10 The Department of Health's central training initiative launched in October 1986 recognises the importance of training for managers and practitioners involved in child abuse work by providing, among other work:

- funding for the production of training videos aimed at doctors and Health Visitors;
- funding for the production by the University of Nottingham of a training pack addressing the difficulties of multi-disciplinary training;
- funding for training at the Department of Post Graduate Training in Child Sexual Abuse at the Institute of Child Health and Great Ormond Street Hospital for Sick Children, London which includes appropriate clinical placements at a number of centres;
- funding for the Open University course P554 'Child Abuse and Neglect: An Introduction' (an individual study pack);
- funding for the NSPCC Training Centre at Leicester, which provides courses for child care workers;
- a training advisory resource (Child Abuse Training Unit) based at the National Children's Bureau.

7.11 Various training materials to explain the provisions of the Children Act in respect of child protection were commissioned and have been published. These include:

(i) Open University course P558;
(ii) National Children's Bureau – 'Child Protection' (a training and practice resource pack);
(iii) National Society for the Prevention of Cruelty to Children – 'Child Protection Adviser's Resource Pack';
(iv) Family Rights Group – 'Working in Partnership with Families'.

7.12 Particular attention should be paid to the Department of Health Guidelines for Trainers and Managers in Social Services Departments Working with Child Sexual Abuse. These guidelines, first issued in 1989, have been revised and are being reissued to accompany this Guide.

7.13 All these publications should be useful for inter-disciplinary training. As further packs are developed, details will be available from the Child Abuse Training Unit.

CASE REVIEWS

INTRODUCTION

8.1 Whenever a case involves an incident leading to the death of a child where child abuse is confirmed or suspected, or a child protection issue likely to be of major public concern arises, there should be an individual review by each agency and a composite review by the ACPC. This includes cases where a child was accommodated by a local authority in a residential setting or with foster carers. Each involved agency should instigate a separate review. Every such case causes distress within the family, creates distress and anxiety among staff of the agencies, and arouses public concern. Agencies need to respond quickly and positively to ensure that their services are maintained and are not undermined by the incident. They also need to ensure that public concern is allayed and media comment is addressed in a positive manner. The timely production of well-conducted case review reports with clear conclusions, and where necessary, positive recommendations for action, should in most cases enable the ACPC and individual agencies to be assured that all necessary lessons are learnt and public concern satisfied.

INFORMATION FOR DEPARTMENT OF HEALTH OR WELSH OFFICE

8.2 Local authorities are required to inform the Department of Health, through SSI in regions, or Welsh Office (as appropriate) immediately they become aware of any case which is covered by paragraph 8.1. This is in addition to the separate requirement (Schedule 2 paragraph 20 of the Children Act) to notify the Secretary of State of the circumstances of the death of any child being looked after by the local authority and of any child who dies in residential care (Regulation 19(2)(c) of the Children's Homes Regulations 1991 S.I. 1991 no 1506). This information should be given by telephone, and subsequently confirmed in writing. The information will provide notice of cases which may arouse acute public concern and allow the Departments to keep guidance in this document under review, and to identify implications for child abuse policy generally. In addition, the Departments will:

- determine whether any particular comment is needed from the centre on matters of professional or other practice in relation to the particular case;

- where necessary, keep under review the implementation of significant recommendations.

8.3 The detailed handling of an individual agency case review will depend on the circumstances of the case and the different organisational structures of the individual agencies. The following paragraphs are intended to cover the general principles and the **review process** in the context of inter-agency co-operation. They do not address the arrangements within individual agencies. ACPCs should consider the need for a standard format for reports to facilitate the production of the ACPC inter-agency report.

GENERAL PRINCIPLES

8.4 The following underlying principles are most important. The degree of relevance will depend upon the nature of the case and type of review:

(a) *Urgency*: Agencies should take action immediately and follow this through as quickly as possible.

(b) *Impartiality*: Those conducting reviews should not have been directly concerned with the child or the family.

(c) *Thoroughness*: All important factors should be considered and there should be an opportunity for all those involved to contribute.

(d) *Openness*: There should be no suspicion of concealment. This means quick and clear communication with elected members and the public.

(e) *Confidentiality*: Due regard must be paid to the balance of individuals' rights and the public interest.

(f) *Co-operation*: The local ACPC should provide a framework to ensure close collaboration between all the agencies involved.

(g) *Resolution*: Action should be taken to implement any recommendations that may arise and are accepted by the agencies concerned.

IMMEDIATE ACTION BY ALL AGENCIES

The Individual Agency Review Process

8.5 As soon as a case as described in paragraph 8.1 above is identified, the identifying agency should immediately ensure that all its files and notes relating to the child are secured. It should also alert the holder of the child protection register and the chair of the ACPC to ensure that all other agencies take similar action. Each agency should carry out an urgent management review to establish:

(a) whether the agency child protection procedures have been followed;

(b) whether the case suggests that there is an urgent need to review those procedures;

(c) whether any other action is needed within the agency.

8.6 The overall purpose of the review by each agency should be to secure the best possible quality of services for children and their families. The specific action should have the following main objectives:

- to establish a factual chronology of the action which has been taken within the agency;

- to assess whether decisions and actions taken in the case appear to have been in line with the policy and procedure within that agency;

- to consider what services were provided in relation to the decisions and actions in the case;

- to recommend appropriate action in the light of the review's findings.

8.7 The initial task of the review is to establish the facts as known to the agency at that time. It is for this reason that it is vital that records relating to the case are immediately secured against interference or loss. It will be necessary to construct a diary of events to obtain a complete picture of the case as seen by the individual agency. The establishment of a comprehensive diary reflecting the involvement of all agencies will follow later. The police should be able to provide factual details of police involvement in the case prior to the incident which gave rise to the review, even if they are not able, for reasons of criminal justice, to share information gained after the incident until any criminal proceedings have been completed.

8.8 Managers will need to ensure that staff directly involved in the case are informed of the purpose of the review and the way it will be conducted. This will help to reduce anxiety and, with management support, enable staff to continue providing a service to their other clients. Trade unions and professional associations and staff not directly involved in the case should also be kept informed of progress. It should be made clear in any such discussions that the review is separate from, even if it leads to, any action necessary under established disciplinary procedures. All those involved will need to be aware that nothing in this Guide prevents an individual agency conducting, or causing to be conducted, any other form of investigation or inquiry at any stage.

8.9 In each agency, the senior officer will need to designate someone to undertake the review. Agencies should ensure that progress is not impeded and arrange, if necessary, appropriate cover for normal duties for the person conducting the review. The health authority and social services committees and parent authorities of other agencies as appropriate will need to be kept informed in accordance with locally agreed procedures.

8.10 It is inevitable that some cases will attract particular public and media interest. Agencies should have a clear policy on, and appoint persons to act as a point of contact with, the media within an agreed ACPC framework. The importance of keeping the media and public informed should be recognised, and there should be close co-operation between agencies on the release of statements. All agencies will need to consult their legal advisers and the police to ensure that nothing is made public in contempt of court or in any way prejudicial to any civil or criminal proceedings.

8.11 Individual agencies should complete their individual (agency) case reviews within one month of the incident occurring. They should then present their report and recommendations for future action to the appropriate authority, who should pass the final version to the ACPC within seven working days. In a few cases it will be obvious that more urgent inter-agency communication will be needed, for instance if there were doubts about the continuing safety of another child, or someone in another agency was implicated in an offence.

Inter-agency Co-operation

8.12 Close co-operation between agencies through the ACPC is important as case reviews are set up and progressed. A complete picture of the events can only be produced in collaboration with other agencies involved. If criminal investigations are proceeding and prosecution is being considered, it will be particularly important for agencies to be aware of the action the police or the prosecuting authorities are undertaking, and vice versa.

8.13 The ACPC should provide a focus for ensuring:

- co-operative and co-ordinated action from the outset;
- that all local agencies that have been, or could have been, involved with the child and family are immediately informed of action planned;
- that the findings of the individual case reviews are brought together to form the overall picture of service provision in the case, and advice attached on the need for any future action.

8.14 The ACPC should agree in advance the most suitable way of undertaking these tasks. It may be helpful either to establish a permanent sub-committee to consider case reviews, or to agree the framework under which a sub-committee can be set up quickly, if and when the need arises. It will be important to inform the Chair of the ACPC of the arrangements in a particular case, including the timetable for completion of the exercise.

8.15 The ACPC should build up a picture of what happened through the individual agency case reviews, having regard to the differing management structures within each agency. The momentum and need for individual case reviews should be maintained notwithstanding police inquiries. The need for action considered by the ACPC should not await the outcome of such inquiries.

URGENT ACPC ACTION

8.16 As soon as the ACPC receives the individual agency reports, urgent action should be taken to identify any discrepancies between the agency reports or other issues requiring immediate attention. These should be communicated to the appropriate agencies at once. Depending on the seriousness of the discrepancies or apparent failure of procedure or potential for continuing harm to other children, the ACPC may need to convene an emergency meeting or take other action. The ACPC should also identify as a matter of urgency whether there is a need to request additional reports from others involved, e.g. a general medical practitioner or the proprietor of a school or registered home.

Production of an Inter-agency Report

8.17 Within three weeks of the appropriate authorities presenting their recommendations to the ACPC, the ACPC should produce an overview report to all agencies setting out the full facts of the case, highlighting actions and issues and making any proposals for change, including an indication of the suggested timescale. The ACPC should also identify any matters requiring further investigation. This should ensure that agencies have clear indications of the situation leading up to a case – as well as the recommendations for future action – within two months of the case arising. The ACPC overview report, which should include the individual agency reports, should be sent to the Department of Health, through SSI in regions, or Welsh Office as appropriate.

Police Action

8.18 The police, on behalf of the coroner, will conduct an investigation into the cause of the death of a child and into whether anybody is criminally responsible for it. Witnesses will be interviewed and written statements obtained. Where the police consider there is sufficient evidence against a person of an offence, they may charge that person and must refer the case to the Crown Prosecution Service (CPS). Thereafter the conduct of the case is undertaken by the CPS, who will decide whether the evidence is sufficient for proceedings and, if so, will arrange for the case to be brought to trial. The coroner's inquest will be adjourned pending the outcome of the prosecution. In other cases involving harm to a child, the police may conduct an investigation and the CPS may prosecute any person whom they consider has committed a criminal offence in respect of the child. The police, through membership of the ACPC, should be kept in touch with the case reviews and should contribute such information to the ACPC as circumstances permit. ACPC action should not be postponed until the police or the CPS have made a decision whether to prosecute.

SUBSEQUENT ACTION

8.19 The aim of the ACPC overview report should be to ensure that any lessons from the events under review are acted upon promptly and effectively. Problems of inter-agency concern should be considered by the ACPC, who will need to monitor and implement the agreed changes, details of which should be published. In the overview report to the agencies on the case reviews, the ACPC should indicate whether there are any aspects of the case which seem to justify further inquiry, either under the auspices of the ACPC or by an individual agency or agencies.

8.20 Inquiries have taken a number of different forms. In an individual case the advice of the Department of Health, the Welsh Office, Home Office or Department of Education and Science (as appropriate) will be available. It will be for the agencies individually or jointly to consider what form an inquiry should take.

8.21 In most cases, the consideration of the case by each individual agency, the sharing of that individual agency's report with other agencies, and the production of an inter-agency overview report of the case will suffice.

Access to Health Record Act 1990. HSG(91)6.

Access to Personal Files Act 1987: Access to Personal Files (Social Services) Regulations. LAC(89)2.

Access to Personal Files (Social Services) Regulations 1989 and local authority social services (Designation of Functions) order 1989. LAC(89)8.

Access to Personal Files (Social Services) (Amendment) Regulations 1991 LAC(91)11.

Child Abuse – A Study of Inquiry Reports 1973–1981 (HMSO 1982; ISBN 0-11-320788-3).

Child Abuse – A Study of Inquiry Reports 1980–1989 (HMSO 1991; ISBN 0-11-321391-3).

Child Care Policy – Putting It in Writing – A Review of English Local Authority Child Care Policy Statements (HMSO 1991).

Child Protection: Working Together. Part 1: The Process of Learning and Training. Part II: Sharing Perspectives. Marian Charles with Olive Stevenson (University of Nottingham).

Child Psychiatry and the Law. Edited by Dora Black, Stephen Wolkind, Jean Harris Hendricks (Royal College of Psychiatrists; ISBN 0-902241-31-1).

Child Protection: Guidance for Senior Nurses, Health Visitors and Midwives. Standing Nursing and Midwifery Advisory Committee report (HMSO; ISBN 0-11-321156-2) (to be updated).

Children in the Public Care. A review of residential care. Sir William Utting (HMSO 1991; ISBN 0-11-321455-3).

Co-ordination and Child Protection: A Review of Literature. Christine Hallett and Elizabeth Birchell (HMSO – to be published spring 1992).

Department of Education and Science circular 4/88 – Working Together for the Protection of Children from Abuse: Procedures within the Education Service.

Diagnosis of Child Sexual Abuse. Guidance for Doctors – Standing Medical Advisory Committee report in July 1988 (ISBN 0-11-321155-4).

The Education (School Records) Regulations 1989 (S.I. 1989/1261) (DES circular 17/89).

Family Court Service Committees (The Lord Chancellor's Department).

Home Office Circular: The Investigation of Child Sexual Abuse (to be issued simultaneously with *Working Together*).

Home Office Circular 54/91: The Children Act 1989.

Joint Training for Police Officers and Social Workers responsible for investigating Child Sexual Abuse (Home Office Circular 67/1989).

Metropolitan Police and Bexley Social Services. Child Sexual Abuse Investigative Experiment Final Report (HMSO 1987; ISBN 0-11-340886-2).

Notification of Deaths of Children in Care and under local authority supervision (LASS 176/19/1).

Patient Consent to Examination or Treatment HC(90)2.

Patterns and Outcomes in Child Placement – Mesages from current research and their implications (HMSO 1991; ISBN 0-11-321357-3).

Physical Signs of Sexual Abuse in Children: a report of the Royal College of Physicians of London (April 1991; ISBN 1-873240-20-1).

Protecting Children – A Guide for social workers undertaking a comprehensive assessment (HMSO 1988; ISBN 0-11-321159-7).

The Care of Children – Principles and Practice in Regulations and Guidance (HMSO 1991; ISBN 0-11-321289-5).

The Children Act 1989 – an introductory guide for the NHS. Department of Health.

The Children Act 1989 Guidance and Regulations. Volume 1 – Court Orders (HMSO 1991; ISBN 0-11-321371-9).

The Children Act 1989 Guidance and Regulations. Volume 2 – Family Support, Day Care and Educational Provision for Young Children (HMSO 1991; ISBN 0-11-321372-7).

The Children Act 1989 Guidance and Regulations. Volume 3 – Family Placements (HMSO 1991; ISBN 0-11-321375-1).

The Children Act 1989 Guidance and Regulations. Volume 4 – Residential Care (HMSO 1991; ISBN 0-11-321430-8).

The Children Act 1989 Guidance and Regulations. Volume 5 – Independent Schools (HMSO 1991; ISBN 0-11-321373-5).

The Children Act 1989 Guidance and Regulations. Volume 6 – Children with Disabilities (HMSO 1991; ISBN 0-11-321452-9).

The Children Act 1989 Guidance and Regulations. Volume 7 – Guardians ad Litem and Other Court-related Issues (HMSO 1991).

The Children Act 1989 Guidance and Regulations. Volume 8 – Private Fostering and Miscellaneous (HMSO 1991).

The Children Act 1989 Guidance and Regulations. Volume 9 – Adoption Issues (HMSO 1991).

The Pindown Experience and the Protection of Children – The Report of the Staffordshire Child Care Inquiry 1990. Staffordshire County Council 1991.

The Report of the Inquiry into Child Abuse in Cleveland 1987 (HMSO 1988; ISBN 0-10-104122-5).

Working with Child Sexual Abuse: Department of Health Guidelines for Trainers and Managers in Social Services Departments (SSI 1991).

THE LEGAL FRAMEWORK

The contents of this Appendix should not be taken as a complete statement of all the relevant legal provisions. It will be necessary to obtain legal advice in relation to every case. Part V of the Children Act 1989 (Protection of Children) is to be found reproduced in its entirety at the end of this Appendix, together with a copy of application forms for emergency protection and child assessment orders in Magistrates' Courts.

The relevant Rules of Court are the Family Proceedings Courts (Children Act 1989) Rules 1991/1395 (Magistrates' Courts) and the Family Proceedings Rules 1991 (S.I. 1991/1247) (County Courts and High Court).

1. General Principles

The Children Act outlines a number of general principles which need to be borne in mind when considering any part of the legal framework:

1.1 The child's welfare shall be the court's paramount consideration. (Section 1(1)).

1.2 The court shall have regard to the general principle that any delay in determining a question with respect to the upbringing of a child is likely to prejudice the welfare of the child. (Section 1(2)).

1.3 The court shall have regard in particular to a number of matters set out in the welfare checklist in Section 1(3) including the wishes and feelings of the child, his age, sex, etc. when considering whether to make, vary or discharge any section 8 order which is opposed, or any order under Part IV.

1.4 Where a child is of sufficient understanding, medical treatment may only be given with his consent (except in medical emergencies). It is for the doctor to decide whether the child is capable of giving consent. Children of 16 and over can give their own consent. Where the child is not of sufficient understanding, the consent of the parent, including a person with parental responsibility, is required. This would include the local authority where the child is subject to a care order. Children who are capable of giving consent cannot be medically examined or assessed without their consent when subject to a child assessment (Section 43), emergency protection (Section 44), or interim care or supervision order (Section 38), or examined, assessed or treated in accordance with a full supervision order (paragraphs 4(4)(a) and 5(5)(a) of Schedule 3) without their consent. If there is a dispute in other circumstances in which a child refuses to consent, the matter should be put to a court to resolve.

1.5 The court shall not make an order unless it considers that doing so would be better for the child then making no order at all. (Section 1(5)).

1.6 For more detailed guidance reference should be made to the Children Act Guidance and Regulations, Volume 1 – Court Orders.

2. Preventive Measures

2.1 There is a duty under Schedule 2, paragraph 1 of the Children Act 1989 to take reasonable steps to identify the extent to which there are children in need within the local authority's area. Under paragraph 4 every local authority has a duty to take reasonable steps by providing services under Part III of the Act to prevent children within their area suffering ill treatment or neglect. There is a duty to share information about any child who is likely to suffer harm between local authorities where appropriate.

2.2 Paragraph 7 provides that every local authority shall take reasonable steps to reduce the need to bring proceedings for care or supervision orders or criminal proceedings in relation to children. Similarly, there is a duty to encourage children not to commit criminal offences and to avoid the need for children in their area to be placed in secure accommodation.

2.3 Section 17 of the Act makes it a general duty of every local authority:

"(a) to safeguard and promote the welfare of children within their area who are in need; and

(b) so far as is consistent with that duty, to promote the upbringing of such children by their families, by providing a range and level of services appropriate to those children's needs."

2.4 Alternatively, they may arrange for others to provide the services. Such assistance may include assistance in kind or, in exceptional circumstances, in cash.

3. Provision of Accommodation for Children

3.1 Section 20 of the Act makes it a duty for every local authority to provide accommodation for any child in need within their area who appears to them to require accommodation as a result of –

"(a) there being no person who has parental responsibility for him;

(b) his being lost or having been abandoned; or

(c) the person who has been caring for him being prevented (whether or not permanently, and for whatever reason) from providing him with suitable accommodation or care."

4. Duties of Local Authorities in Relation to Children Looked After by Them

4.1 Section 22(3) provides that:

"It shall be the duty of a local authority looking after any child –

(a) to safeguard and promote his welfare; and

(b) to make such use of services available for children cared for by their own parents as appears to the authority reasonable in his case."

4.2 Under Section 22(4) it is the local authority's duty, so far as reasonably practicable, before making any decision in relation to a child to –

"ascertain the wishes and feelings of –

(a) the child;

(b) his parents;

(c) any person who is not a parent of his but who has parental responsibility for him; and

(d) any other person whose wishes and feelings the authority consider to be relevant, regarding the matter to be decided."

4.3 Section 22(5) provides that in making such a decision the local authority must give due consideration to the child's age and understanding and wishes, anyone else they have consulted, and the child's "religious persuasion, racial origin and cultural and linguistic background".

4.4 Section 23 provides that the local authority must accommodate (as most appropriate) and maintain such children.

4.5 It is also the local authority's duty to provide after care for young persons over 16 who have been looked after by them up to the age of 21. Section 24(1) provides –

"where a child is being looked after by a local authority, it shall be the duty of the authority to advise, assist and befriend with a view to promoting his welfare when he ceases to be looked after by them."

5. Review of Cases

5.1 Section 26 of the Act and the Review of Children's Cases Regulations 1991 (S.I. 1991 No. 895) provide for the cases of all children being looked after by local authorities to be regularly reviewed at specified periods.

6. Representation Procedure

6.1 Section 26(3) of the Act provides that every local authority shall establish a procedure for considering any representations (including any complaint) made to them by the persons specified in (a) to (e) about the discharge by the authority of any of their functions under Part III in relation to the child.

6.2 The procedure involves consideration of the matter by an independent person and a Panel which also includes an independent person. The Representations Procedure (Children) Regulations 1991 (S.I. No. 894) set out further requirements.

7. Duty to Investigate

7.1 Section 37 provides that:

"Where, in any family proceedings in which a question arises with respect to the welfare of any child, it appears to the court that it may be appropriate for a care or supervision order to be made with respect to him, the court may direct the appropriate authority to undertake an investigation of the child's circumstances."

The authority must then investigate and consider whether it would be appropriate to apply for a care or supervision order, or to provide services or other help for the child and his family, or to take some other action. If they decide not to apply for a care or supervision order, they must give the court their reasons and tell them what they are doing instead within 8 weeks unless the court directs otherwise.

7.2 Section 47(1) gives the local authority a duty to investigate where they –

"(a) are informed that a child who lives, or is found, in their area –

(i) is the subject of an emergency protection order; or

(ii) is in police protection; or

(b) have reasonable cause to suspect that a child who lives, or is found, in their area is suffering, or is likely to suffer, significant harm,

the authority shall make, or cause to make, such enquiries as they consider necessary to enable them to decide whether they should take any action to safeguard or promote the child's welfare". This includes obtaining access to him. If access is denied or information withheld they must take reasonable steps to obtain access or information unless they are satisfied they already have sufficient information. They may call upon other local authorities, health authorities, education authorities, etc. for assistance and it shall be the duty of such authorities to assist unless it would be unreasonable in the circumstances.

7.3 This supplements the earlier provision in Section 26(3) of the National Health Service Act 1977 which provides that the Secretary of State shall make available to local authorities the services provided by health authorities as part of the health service so far as reasonably necessary and practicable to enable them to discharge (amongst others) their social services functions. Section 3(1) of the Health Services Act 1984 extends this so that GPs' services are also available. The same applies when the authority itself has taken out an emergency protection order.

7.4 Section 47(8) provides that where as a result of such enquiry they conclude that they should take some action, they must do so, so far as is practicable.

Grounds

8.1 A care order under Section 31 of the Act may only be made by a court if it is satisfied –

"(a) that the child concerned is suffering, or is likely to suffer, significant harm; and

(b) that the harm, or likelihood of harm, is attributable to –

    (i) the care given to the child, or likely to be given to him if the order were not made, not being what it would be reasonable to expect a parent to give to him; or

    (ii) the child's being beyond parental control."

Care Orders

8.2 Where a care order has been made, Section 33 of the Act gives the local authority designated in the order parental responsibility for the child in addition to the parents. Where they are satisfied that it is necessary to do so in order to safeguard or promote the child's welfare the local authority has the power to determine the extent to which a parent or guardian of the child may meet his parental responsibility for him. Nonetheless a parent or guardian who has care of the child may still do what is reasonable in all the circumstances of the case to safeguard or promote the child's welfare.

8.3 The local authority shall not cause the child to be brought up in any religious persuasion other than that in which he would have been brought up if the order had not been made, nor consent or refuse to consent to an adoption application, nor appoint a guardian for the child. No one has the right to change the child's surname or remove him from the United Kingdom without the written consent of every person with parental responsibility for the child or by order of the court.

8.4 Care orders may be discharged by the court under Section 39 on the application of any person with parental responsibility, the child himself or the relevant local authority. The court may substitute a supervision order on such an application. The care order is also discharged on the making of a residence order under Section 8.

Supervision Orders

8.5 Under Section 31 of the Act –

"on the application of any local authority or authorised person, the court may make an order –

(a) placing the child with respect to whom the application is made in the care of a designated local authroity;

(b) putting him under the supervision of a designated local authority or of a probation officer."

8.6 The criteria for making a supervision order are the same as for a care order. No supervision order may be made with respect to a child who is 17 or over (or 16 if he is married).

8.7 Section 35 sets out the duties of a supervisor:

"while a supervision order is in force it shall be the duty of the supervisor –

(a) to advise, assist and befriend the supervised child;

(b) to take such steps as are reasonably necessary to give effect to the order; and

(c) where –

    (i) the order is not wholly complied with; or

    (ii) the supervisor considers that the order may no longer be necessary,

to consider whether or not to apply to the court for its variation or discharge."

8.8 Schedule 3, Parts I and II make further provision for supervision orders. Paragraph 2 sets out the powers of the supervisor to give directions to the child:

"A supervision order may require the supervised child to comply with any directions given from time to time by the supervisor which require him to do all or any of the following things –

(a) to live at a place or places specified in the directions for a period or period so specified;

(b) to present himself to a person or persons specified in the directions at a place or places or on a day or days so specified;

(c) to participate in activities specified in the directions on a day or day so specified."

It is for the supervisor to decide whether, and to what extent, he exercises any power, afforded by the order, to give directions.

8.9 Provisions relating to psychiatric and medical examinations are set out in paragraphs 4 and 5 of Schedule 3. The supervisor may make directions on medical and psychiatric examinations only where the supervision order includes a requirement that the child submits to such an examination from time to time as directed by the supervisor. Directions about medical or psychiatric treatment can be made by the court only and should be set out in the supervision order. Where the child has sufficient understanding to make an informed decision, his consent is needed to include any directions about medical and psychiatric examination or treatment in the supervision order.

8.10 A supervision order may be varied or discharged by the court under Section 39 on the application of –

"(a) any person who has parental responsibility for the child; (not, for example, a father who does not have parental responsibility);

(b) the child himself; or

(c) the supervisor."

A care order may be substituted for a supervision order.

8.11 A supervision order ceases to have effect at the end of a year after the date it was made, under paragraph 6 of Schedule 3. A supervisor may apply to the court to have this period extended for such period as the court may specify but not so as to run beyond a period of 3 years from the date when it was first made.

9. Contact with Children in Care

9.1 Section 34 provides that:

"where a child is in the care of a local authority, the authority shall (subject to the provisions of this section) allow the child reasonable contact with –

(a) his parents;

(b) any guardian of his;

(c) where there was a residence order in force with respect to the child immediately before the care order was made, the person in whose favour the order was made; and

(d) where, immediately before the care order was made, a person had care of the child by virtue of an order made in the exercise of the High Court's inherent jurisdiction with respect to children, that person."

Other people may make applications for contact with the child if they obtained the leave of the court first.

9.2 If the authority want to refuse to allow contact between the child and any person mentioned in (a) to (d) above, they must apply to the court for an order. In an emergency an authority may refuse to allow contact without an order from the court if they are satisfied that it is necessary to do so in order to safeguard or promote the child's welfare, and the refusal is decided upon as a matter of urgency and does not last for more than 7 days. A contact order may be varied or discharged by the court on the application of the authority, the child concerned or the person named in the order.

10. Interim Orders

10.1 Section 38 of the Act provides that an interim care order or supervision order may be made by the court:

"a court shall not make an interim care order or interim supervision order under this section unless it is satisfied that there are reasonable grounds for believing that the circumstances with respect to the child are as mentioned in Section 31(2)."

10.2 An interim order may not last initially for more than 8 weeks. A second or subsequent such order made with respect to the same child in the same proceedings may not last more than 4 weeks or 8 weeks from the date of the original order if this is later. The order may specify such lesser period as is appropriate. It will also cease if the application is disposed of sooner. The court may give such directions as it considers appropriate with regard to medical or psychiatric examination or other assessment of the child, though the child may refuse to submit to such an examination if he is of sufficient understanding to make an informed decision.

11. Emergency Procedures

11.1 Section 44 provides that orders for emergency protection of children may only be made if the court is satisfied that –

"(a) there is reasonable cause to believe that the child is likely to suffer significant harm if –

   (i)   he is not removed to accommodation provided by or on behalf of the applicant; or

   (ii) he does not remain in the place in which he is then being accommodated;

 (b) in the case of an application made by a local authority –

   (i)   enquiries are being made with respect to the child under Section 47(1)(b); and

   (ii) those enquiries are being frustrated by access to the child being unreasonably refused to a person authorised to seek access and that the applicant has reasonable cause to believe that access to the child is required as a matter of urgency".

A similar requirement is necessary where the application is made by an authorised person as defined in Section 31(9) of the Act. Such order may only last for 8 days. The court may exceptionally extend it for a further period not exceeding 7 days, but only once.

11.2 The effect of an EPO is to give parental responsibility to the local authority in addition to the parents or whoever had it immediately before. The order may order that the child be removed or kept where he is, and may give directions about medical examinations or assessment. It may give directions about contact. An order to remove the child will only be made if necessary and he should be returned when it is safe to do so.

11.3 Section 45(8) provides that an application may be made to discharge the emergency protection order after the expiry of 72 hours from making the order by the child, his parent, anyone with parental responsibility, or anyone with whom he was living immediately before unless they were given notice (in accordance with the Rules of Court) of the hearing at which the order was made and were present at the hearing. No application can be made for discharge once the original period of the order has been extended by the court.

11.4 Section 46 authorises a police constable to remove the child to suitable accommodation and keep him there or take such steps as are reasonable to prevent the child's removal from some place. No child may be kept in police protection for more than 72 hours. The police must take steps as soon as reasonably practicable to inform the child's parents of what he has done and the reasons for it and what he intends to do next and shall also inform the local authority of what he has done and the reasons for it. If the child appears capable of understanding he must also be so informed. The police can apply for an emergency protection order on behalf of a local authority whether or not the authority know or agree. (Section 46(8).)

11.5 Section 48(1) provides that where it appears to a court making an emergency protection order that –

"adequate information as to the child's whereabouts –

(a) is not available to the applicant for the order; but

(b) is available to another person,

it may include in the order a provision requiring that other person to disclose, if asked to do so by the applicant, any information that he may have as to the child's whereabouts."

11.6 Under Section 48(3) and (4) the order may also authorise the applicant to enter premises specified in the order and search for another child if the court has reasonable cause to believe that he may be on the premises. Section 48(7) makes it an offence to obstruct the implementation of such order. The court may also grant a warrant authorising a constable to assist the applicant exercising his emergency protection powers using reasonable force if necessary. Section 48(11) permits a court that a constable may be accompanied by a doctor, registered nurse or registered health visitor if he so chooses.

11.7 Section 48(13) provides that where possible the warrant shall name the child, and if it does not it shall describe him as clearly as possible.

11.8 Section 50 provides for the court to make a recovery order where there is reason to believe that children in care have been abducted, have run away or are missing. A recovery order authorises a constable to enter any premises specified in the order to search for the child, the removal of the child by an authorised person, requires anyone with information about the child to disclose it to a constable if asked to do so and operates as a direction to anyone who is in a position to do so to produce the child on request to an authorised person. An authorised person is defined in Section 50(7) and includes any constable and anyone authorised by the court.

12. Child Assessment Orders

Section 43(1) provides that:

"On the application of a local authority or authorised person for an order to be made under this section with respect to a child, the court may make the order if, but only if, it is satisfied that –

(a) the applicant has reasonable cause to suspect that the child is suffering, or is likely to suffer, significant harm;

(b) an assessment of the state of the child's health or development, or of the way in which he has been treated, is required to enable the applicant to determine whether or not the child is suffering, or is likely to suffer, significant harm; and

(c) it is unlikely that such an assessment will be made, or be satisfactory, in the absence of an order under this section."

An "authorised person" means a person authorised for the purposes of Section 31.

Notice of the hearing must be given to the persons specified in Section 43(11).

The order must specify the date by which the assessment is to begin and have effect for no longer than 7 days from that date.

The order may contain directions, including one to keep the child away from home, and in that case, what contact he is to be allowed with parents, etc. while away from home.

A court may make an emergency protection order instead if it is satisfied that these are grounds for doing so.

13. Section 8 Orders

13.1 *Section 8* introduces four new orders:

- "a contact order" means an order requiring the person with whom a child lives, or is to live, to allow the child to visit or stay with the person named in the order, or for that person and the child otherwise to have contact with each other;

- "a prohibited steps order" means an order that no step which could be taken by a parent in meeting his parental responsibility for a child, and which is of a kind specified in the order, shall be taken by any person without the consent of the court;

- "a residence order" means an order settling the arrangements to be made as to the person with whom a child is to live; and

- "a specific issue order" means an order giving directions for the purpose of determining a specific question which has arisen, or which may arise, in connection with any aspect of parental responsibility for a child.

Any of these may be made by the court of its own motion.

13.2 Section 9 sets out a number of restrictions on the making of Section 8 orders. In particular, only a residence order is available where the child is in care, and this has the effect of discharging the care order (Section 91(1).

The only orders for which a local authority may apply are specific issue(s) and prohibited steps orders (Section 9(2) prohibits applications for residence or contact orders). Section 9(5) provides that a court may not make a specific issue or prohibited steps order if the same result could be achieved by making a residence or contact order or in a way denied to the High Court in the exercise of its inherent jurisdiction with respect to children by Section 100(2).

Only in exceptional cases can a court make any Section 8 order in respect of a child of 16 or over.

Section 10(4) and (5) specifies the person who may apply to the court for a Section 8 order. Other people may apply with leave of the court. Section 10(9) sets out particular matters to which the court should have regard when deciding whether to grant leave.

13.3 Section 11(7) provides that a Section 8 order may contain directions about how it is to be carried into effect and impose conditions.

14. Family Assistance Orders

Section 16 provides that:

"Where, in any family proceedings, the court has power to make an order under this Part with respect to any child, it may (whether or not it makes such an order) make an order requiring –

(a) a probation officer to be made available; or

(b) a local authority to make an officer of the authority available, to advise, assist and (where appropriate) befriend any person named in the order".

These may only be used in exceptional cases with the consent of all parties, excluding the child, and on the court's own motion. It may not last more than 6 months.

15.1 Under Section 41 the court shall appoint a guardian ad litem for the child concerned in specified proceedings unless the court is satisfied that it is not necessary to safeguard the child's interests.

15.2 The specified proceedings are listed in Section 41(6) and augmented by the Rules of Court. They include any application for care or supervision orders or an emergency protection order.

15.3 The guardian's duty is to safeguard the interests of the child as described in the Rules of Court. The Rules make further provision as to the guardian's role.

15.4 Guardians will be selected from panels. Provisions about these panels, their constitution, qualifications for members, training, etc. are contained in the Guardian ad Litem and Reporting Officers (Panels) Regulations 1991.

15.5 Guardians have the right to examine and take copies of local authority records relating to the child (Section 42). Copies taken are admissible as evidence in the report he makes to the court and any evidence he gives in proceedings, regardless of anything which might otherwise make the evidence inadmissible.

PART V

PROTECTION OF CHILDREN

43.—(1) On the application of a local authority or authorised person for an order to be made under this section with respect to a child, the court may make the order if, but only if, it is satisfied that—

>   (a) the applicant has reasonable cause to suspect that the child is suffering, or is likely to suffer, significant harm;

>   (b) an assessment of the state of the child's health or development, or of the way in which he has been treated, is required to enable the applicant to determine whether or not the child is suffering, or is likely to suffer, significant harm; and

>   (c) it is unlikely that such an assessment will be made, or be satisfactory, in the absence of an order under this section.

(2) In this Act "a child assessment order" means an order under this section.

(3) A court may treat an application under this section as an application for an emergency protection order.

(4) No court shall make a child assessment order if it is satisfied—

>   (a) that there are grounds for making an emergency protection order with respect to the child; and

>   (b) that it ought to make such an order rather than a child assessment order.

(5) A child assessment order shall—

>   (a) specify the date by which the assessment is to begin; and

>   (b) have effect for such period, not exceeding 7 days beginning with that date, as may be specified in the order.

(6) Where a child assessment order is in force with respect to a child it shall be the duty of any person who is in a position to produce the child—

>   (a) to produce him to such person as may be named in the order; and

>   (b) to comply with such directions relating to the assessment of the child as the court thinks fit to specify in the order.

(7) A child assessment order authorises any person carrying out the assessment, or any part of the assessment, to do so in accordance with the terms of the order.

(8) Regardless of subsection (7), if the child is of sufficient understanding to make an informed decision he may refuse to submit to a medical or psychiatric examination or other assessment.

(9) The child may only be kept away from home—

>   (a) in accordance with directions specified in the order;

>   (b) if it is necessary for the purposes of the assessment; and

>   (c) for such period or periods as may be specified in the order.

(10) Where the child is to be kept away from home, the order shall contain such directions as the court thinks fit with regard to the contact that he must be allowed to have with other persons while away from home.

(11) Any person making an application for a child assessment order shall take such steps as are reasonably practicable to ensure that notice of

PART V the application is given to—

(a) the child's parents;

(b) any person who is not a parent of his but who has parental responsibility for him;

(c) any other person caring for the child;

(d) any person in whose favour a contact order is in force with respect to the child;

(e) any person who is allowed to have contact with the child by virtue of an order under section 34; and

(f) the child,

before the hearing of the application.

(12) Rules of court may make provision as to the circumstances in which—

(a) any of the persons mentioned in subsection (11); or

(b) such other person as may be specified in the rules,

may apply to the court for a child assessment order to be varied or discharged.

(13) In this section "authorised person" means a person who is an authorised person for the purposes of section 31.

Orders for emergency protection of children.

44.—(1) Where any person ("the applicant") applies to the court for an order to be made under this section with respect to a child, the court may make the order if, but only if, it is satisfied that—

(a) there is reasonable cause to believe that the child is likely to suffer significant harm if—

(i) he is not removed to accommodation provided by or on behalf of the applicant; or

(ii) he does not remain in the place in which he is then being accommodated;

(b) in the case of an application made by a local authority—

(i) enquiries are being made with respect to the child under section 47(1)(b); and

(ii) those enquiries are being frustrated by access to the child being unreasonably refused to a person authorised to seek access and that the applicant has reasonable cause to believe that access to the child is required as a matter of urgency; or

(c) in the case of an application made by an authorised person—

(i) the applicant has reasonable cause to suspect that a child is suffering, or is likely to suffer, significant harm;

(ii) the applicant is making enquiries with respect to the child's welfare; and

(iii) those enquiries are being frustrated by access to the child being unreasonably refused to a person authorised to seek access and the applicant has reasonable cause to believe that access to the child is required as a matter of urgency.

(2) In this section—

(a) "authorised person" means a person who is an authorised person for the purposes of section 31; and

(b) "a person authorised to seek access" means—

(i) in the case of an application by a local authority, an officer of the local authority or a person authorised by the authority to act on their behalf in connection with the enquiries; or

(ii) in the case of an application by an authorised person, that person.

(3) Any person—

(a) seeking access to a child in connection with enquiries of a kind mentioned in subsection (1); and

(b) purporting to be a person authorised to do so,

shall, on being asked to do so, produce some duly authenticated document as evidence that he is such a person.

(4) While an order under this section ("an emergency protection order") is in force it—

(a) operates as a direction to any person who is in a position to do so to comply with any request to produce the child to the applicant;

(b) authorises—

(i) the removal of the child at any time to accommodation provided by or on behalf of the applicant and his being kept there; or

(ii) the prevention of the child's removal from any hospital, or other place, in which he was being accommodated immediately before the making of the order; and

(c) gives the applicant parental responsibility for the child.

(5) Where an emergency protection order is in force with respect to a child, the applicant—

(a) shall only exercise the power given by virtue of subsection (4)(b) in order to safeguard the welfare of the child;

(b) shall take, and shall only take, such action in meeting his parental responsibility for the child as is reasonably required to safeguard or promote the welfare of the child (having regard in particular to the duration of the order); and

(c) shall comply with the requirements of any regulations made by the Secretary of State for the purposes of this subsection.

(6) Where the court makes an emergency protection order, it may give such directions (if any) as it considers appropriate with respect to—

(a) the contact which is, or is not, to be allowed between the child and any named person;

(b) the medical or psychiatric examination or other assessment of the child.

(7) Where any direction is given under subsection (6)(b), the child may, if he is of sufficient understanding to make an informed decision, refuse to submit to the examination or other assessment.

(8) A direction under subsection (6)(a) may impose conditions and one under subsection (6)(b) may be to the effect that there is to be—

(a) no such examination or assessment; or

(b) no such examination or assessment unless the court directs otherwise.

(9) A direction under subsection (6) may be—

(a) given when the emergency protection order is made or at any time while it is in force; and

(b) varied at any time on the application of any person falling within any class of person prescribed by rules of court for the purposes of this subsection.

(10) Where an emergency protection order is in force with respect to a child and—

(a) the applicant has exercised the power given by subsection (4)(b)(i) but it appears to him that it is safe for the child to be returned; or

(b) the applicant has exercised the power given by subsection (4)(b)(ii) but it appears to him that it is safe for the child to be allowed to be removed from the place in question,

he shall return the child or (as the case may be) allow him to be removed.

(11) Where he is required by subsection (10) to return the child the applicant shall—

(a) return him to the care of the person from whose care he was removed; or

(b) if that is not reasonably practicable, return him to the care of—

(i) a parent of his;

(ii) any person who is not a parent of his but who has parental responsibility for him; or

(iii) such other person as the applicant (with the agreement of the court) considers appropriate.

(12) Where the applicant has been required by subsection (10) to return the child, or to allow him to be removed, he may again exercise his powers with respect to the child (at any time while the emergency protection order remains in force) if it appears to him that a change in the circumstances of the case makes it necessary for him to do so.

(13) Where an emergency protection order has been made with respect to a child, the applicant shall, subject to any direction given under subsection (6), allow the child reasonable contact with—

(a) his parents;

(b) any person who is not a parent of his but who has parental responsibility for him;

(c) any person with whom he was living immediately before the making of the order;

(d) any person in whose favour a contact order is in force with respect to him;

(e) any person who is allowed to have contact with the child by virtue of an order under section 34; and

(f) any person acting on behalf of any of those persons.

(14) Wherever it is reasonably practicable to do so, an emergency protection order shall name the child; and where it does not name him it shall describe him as clearly as possible.

(15) A person shall be guilty of an offence if he intentionally obstructs

any person exercising the power under subsection (4)(b) to remove, or prevent the removal of, a child.

(16) A person guilty of an offence under subsection (15) shall be liable on summary conviction to a fine not exceeding level 3 on the standard scale.

45.—(1) An emergency protection order shall have effect for such period, not exceeding eight days, as may be specified in the order.

(2) Where—

    (a) the court making an emergency protection order would, but for this subsection, specify a period of eight days as the period for which the order is to have effect; but

    (b) the last of those eight days is a public holiday (that is to say, Christmas Day, Good Friday, a bank holiday or a Sunday),

the court may specify a period which ends at noon on the first later day which is not such a holiday.

(3) Where an emergency protection order is made on an application under section 46(7), the period of eight days mentioned in subsection (1) shall begin with the first day on which the child was taken into police protection under section 46.

(4) Any person who—

    (a) has parental responsibility for a child as the result of an emergency protection order; and

    (b) is entitled to apply for a care order with respect to the child,

may apply to the court for the period during which the emergency protection order is to have effect to be extended.

(5) On an application under subsection (4) the court may extend the period during which the order is to have effect by such period, not exceeding seven days, as it thinks fit, but may do so only if it has reasonable cause to believe that the child concerned is likely to suffer significant harm if the order is not extended.

(6) An emergency protection order may only be extended once.

(7) Regardless of any enactment or rule of law which would otherwise prevent it from doing so, a court hearing an application for, or with respect to, an emergency protection order may take account of—

    (a) any statement contained in any report made to the court in the course of, or in connection with, the hearing; or

    (b) any evidence given during the hearing,

which is, in the opinion of the court, relevant to the application.

(8) Any of the following may apply to the court for an emergency protection order to be discharged—

    (a) the child;

    (b) a parent of his;

    (c) any person who is not a parent of his but who has parental responsibility for him; or

    (d) any person with whom he was living immediately before the making of the order.

(9) No application for the discharge of an emergency protection order shall be heard by the court before the expiry of the period of 72 hours beginning with the making of the order.

Duration of emergency protection orders and other supplemental provisions.

PART V

(10) No appeal may be made against the making of, or refusal to make, an emergency protection order or against any direction given by the court in connection with such an order.

(11) Subsection (8) does not apply—

(a) where the person who would otherwise be entitled to apply for the emergency protection order to be discharged—

(i) was given notice (in accordance with rules of court) of the hearing at which the order was made; and

(ii) was present at that hearing; or

(b) to any emergency protection order the effective period of which has been extended under subsection (5).

(12) A court making an emergency protection order may direct that the applicant may, in exercising any powers which he has by virtue of the order, be accompanied by a registered medical practitioner, registered nurse or registered health visitor, if he so chooses.

Removal and accommodation of children by police in cases of emergency.

46.—(1) Where a constable has reasonable cause to believe that a child would otherwise be likely to suffer significant harm, he may—

(a) remove the child to suitable accommodation and keep him there; or

(b) take such steps as are reasonable to ensure that the child's removal from any hospital, or other place, in which he is then being accommodated is prevented.

(2) For the purposes of this Act, a child with respect to whom a constable has exercised his powers under this section is referred to as having been taken into police protection.

(3) As soon as is reasonably practicable after taking a child into police protection, the constable concerned shall—

(a) inform the local authority within whose area the child was found of the steps that have been, and are proposed to be, taken with respect to the child under this section and the reasons for taking them;

(b) give details to the authority within whose area the child is ordinarily resident ("the appropriate authority") of the place at which the child is being accommodated;

(c) inform the child (if he appears capable of understanding)—

(i) of the steps that have been taken with respect to him under this section and of the reasons for taking them; and

(ii) of the further steps that may be taken with respect to him under this section;

(d) take such steps as are reasonably practicable to discover the wishes and feelings of the child;

(e) secure that the case is inquired into by an officer designated for the purposes of this section by the chief officer of the police area concerned; and

(f) where the child was taken into police protection by being removed to accommodation which is not provided—

(i) by or on behalf of a local authority; or

(ii) as a refuge, in compliance with the requirements of section 51,

secure that he is moved to accommodation which is so provided.

(4) As soon as is reasonably practicable after taking a child into police protection, the constable concerned shall take such steps as are reasonably practicable to inform—

(a) the child's parents;

(b) every person who is not a parent of his but who has parental responsibility for him; and

(c) any other person with whom the child was living immediately before being taken into police protection,

of the steps that he has taken under this section with respect to the child, the reasons for taking them and the further steps that may be taken with respect to him under this section.

(5) On completing any inquiry under subsection (3)(e), the officer conducting it shall release the child from police protection unless he considers that there is still reasonable cause for believing that the child would be likely to suffer significant harm if released.

(6) No child may be kept in police protection for more than 72 hours.

(7) While a child is being kept in police protection, the designated officer may apply on behalf of the appropriate authority for an emergency protection order to be made under section 44 with respect to the child.

(8) An application may be made under subsection (7) whether or not the authority know of it or agree to its being made.

(9) While a child is being kept in police protection—

(a) neither the constable concerned nor the designated officer shall have parental responsibility for him; but

(b) the designated officer shall do what is reasonable in all the circumstances of the case for the purpose of safeguarding or promoting the child's welfare (having regard in particular to the length of the period during which the child will be so protected).

(10) Where a child has been taken into police protection, the designated officer shall allow—

(a) the child's parents;

(b) any person who is not a parent of the child but who has parental responsibility for him;

(c) any person with whom the child was living immediately before he was taken into police protection;

(d) any person in whose favour a contact order is in force with respect to the child;

(e) any person who is allowed to have contact with the child by virtue of an order under section 34; and

(f) any person acting on behalf of any of those persons,

to have such contact (if any) with the child as, in the opinion of the designated officer, is both reasonable and in the child's best interests.

(11) Where a child who has been taken into police protection is in accommodation provided by, or on behalf of, the appropriate authority, subsection (10) shall have effect as if it referred to the authority rather than to the designated officer.

47.—(1) Where a local authority—

(a) are informed that a child who lives, or is found, in their area—

(i) is the subject of an emergency protection order; or

(ii) is in police protection; or

Local authority's duty to investigate.

(b) have reasonable cause to suspect that a child who lives, or is found, in their area is suffering, or is likely to suffer, significant harm,

the authority shall make, or cause to be made, such enquiries as they consider necessary to enable them to decide whether they should take any action to safeguard or promote the child's welfare.

(2) Where a local authority have obtained an emergency protection order with respect to a child, they shall make, or cause to be made, such enquiries as they consider necessary to enable them to decide what action they should take to safeguard or promote the child's welfare.

(3) The enquiries shall, in particular, be directed towards establishing—

(a) whether the authority should make any application to the court, or exercise any of their other powers under this Act, with respect to the child;

(b) whether, in the case of a child—

(i) with respect to whom an emergency protection order has been made; and

(ii) who is not in accommodation provided by or on behalf of the authority,

it would be in the child's best interests (while an emergency protection order remains in force) for him to be in such accommodation; and

(c) whether, in the case of a child who has been taken into police protection, it would be in the child's best interests for the authority to ask for an application to be made under section 46(7).

(4) Where enquiries are being made under subsection (1) with respect to a child, the local authority concerned shall (with a view to enabling them to determine what action, if any, to take with respect to him) take such steps as are reasonably practicable—

(a) to obtain access to him; or

(b) to ensure that access to him is obtained, on their behalf, by a person authorised by them for the purpose,

unless they are satisfied that they already have sufficient information with respect to him.

(5) Where, as a result of any such enquiries, it appears to the authority that there are matters connected with the child's education which should be investigated, they shall consult the relevant local education authority.

(6) Where, in the course of enquiries made under this section—

(a) any officer of the local authority concerned; or

(b) any person authorised by the authority to act on their behalf in connection with those enquiries—

(i) is refused access to the child concerned; or

(ii) is denied information as to his whereabouts,

the authority shall apply for an emergency protection order, a child assessment order, a care order or a supervision order with respect to the child unless they are satisfied that his welfare can be satisfactorily safeguarded without their doing so.

(7) If, on the conclusion of any enquiries or review made under this section, the authority decide not to apply for an emergency protection

order, a child assessment order, a care order or a supervision order they shall—

    (a) consider whether it would be appropriate to review the case at a later date; and

    (b) if they decide that it would be, determine the date on which that review is to begin.

(8) Where, as a result of complying with this section, a local authority conclude that they should take action to safeguard or promote the child's welfare they shall take that action (so far as it is both within their power and reasonably practicable for them to do so).

(9) Where a local authority are conducting enquiries under this section, it shall be the duty of any person mentioned in subsection (11) to assist them with those enquiries (in particular by providing relevant information and advice) if called upon by the authority to do so.

(10) Subsection (9) does not oblige any person to assist a local authority where doing so would be unreasonable in all the circumstances of the case.

(11) The persons are—

    (a) any local authority;

    (b) any local education authority;

    (c) any local housing authority;

    (d) any health authority; and

    (e) any person authorised by the Secretary of State for the purposes of this section.

(12) Where a local authority are making enquiries under this section with respect to a child who appears to them to be ordinarily resident within the area of another authority, they shall consult that other authority, who may undertake the necessary enquiries in their place.

48.—(1) Where it appears to a court making an emergency protection order that adequate information as to the child's whereabouts—   Powers to assist in discovery of children who may be in need of emergency protection.

    (a) is not available to the applicant for the order; but

    (b) is available to another person,

it may include in the order a provision requiring that other person to disclose, if asked to do so by the applicant, any information that he may have as to the child's whereabouts.

(2) No person shall be excused from complying with such a requirement on the ground that complying might incriminate him or his spouse of an offence; but a statement or admission made in complying shall not be admissible in evidence against either of them in proceedings for any offence other than perjury.

(3) An emergency protection order may authorise the applicant to enter premises specified by the order and search for the child with respect to whom the order is made.

(4) Where the court is satisfied that there is reasonable cause to believe that there may be another child on those premises with respect to whom an emergency protection order ought to be made, it may make an order authorising the applicant to search for that other child on those premises.

(5) Where—

    (a) an order has been made under subsection (4);

(b) the child concerned has been found on the premises; and

(c) the applicant is satisfied that the grounds for making an emergency protection order exist with respect to him,

the order shall have effect as if it were an emergency protection order.

(6) Where an order has been made under subsection (4), the applicant shall notify the court of its effect.

(7) A person shall be guilty of an offence if he intentionally obstructs any person exercising the power of entry and search under subsection (3) or (4).

(8) A person guilty of an offence under subsection (7) shall be liable on summary conviction to a fine not exceeding level 3 on the standard scale.

(9) Where, on an application made by any person for a warrant under this section, it appears to the court—

(a) that a person attempting to exercise powers under an emergency protection order has been prevented from doing so by being refused entry to the premises concerned or access to the child concerned; or

(b) that any such person is likely to be so prevented from exercising any such powers,

it may issue a warrant authorising any constable to assist the person mentioned in paragraph (a) or (b) in the exercise of those powers, using reasonable force if necessary.

(10) Every warrant issued under this section shall be addressed to, and executed by, a constable who shall be accompanied by the person applying for the warrant if—

(a) that person so desires; and

(b) the court by whom the warrant is issued does not direct otherwise.

(11) A court granting an application for a warrant under this section may direct that the constable concerned may, in executing the warrant, be accompanied by a registered medical practitioner, registered nurse or registered health visitor if he so chooses.

(12) An application for a warrant under this section shall be made in the manner and form prescribed by rules of court.

(13) Wherever it is reasonably practicable to do so, an order under subsection (4), an application for a warrant under this section and any such warrant shall name the child; and where it does not name him it shall describe him as clearly as possible.

Abduction of children in care etc.

49.—(1) A person shall be guilty of an offence if, knowingly and without lawful authority or reasonable excuse, he—

(a) takes a child to whom this section applies away from the responsible person;

(b) keeps such a child away from the responsible person; or

(c) induces, assists or incites such a child to run away or stay away from the responsible person.

(2) This section applies in relation to a child who is—

(a) in care;

(b) the subject of an emergency protection order; or

(c) in police protection,

and in this section "the responsible person" means any person who for the time being has care of him by virtue of the care order, the emergency protection order, or section 46, as the case may be.

(3) A person guilty of an offence under this section shall be liable on summary conviction to imprisonment for a term not exceeding six months, or to a fine not exceeding level 5 on the standard scale, or to both.

50.—(1) Where it appears to the court that there is reason to believe Recovery of that a child to whom this section applies—   abducted
children etc.

   (a) has been unlawfully taken away or is being unlawfully kept away from the responsible person;

   (b) has run away or is staying away from the responsible person; or

   (c) is missing,

the court may make an order under this section ("a recovery order").

(2) This section applies to the same children to whom section 49 applies and in this section "the responsible person" has the same meaning as in section 49.

(3) A recovery order—

   (a) operates as a direction to any person who is in a position to do so to produce the child on request to any authorised person;

   (b) authorises the removal of the child by any authorised person;

   (c) requires any person who has information as to the child's whereabouts to disclose that information, if asked to do so, to a constable or an officer of the court;

   (d) authorises a constable to enter any premises specified in the order and search for the child, using reasonable force if necessary.

(4) The court may make a recovery order only on the application of—

   (a) any person who has parental responsibility for the child by virtue of a care order or emergency protection order; or

   (b) where the child is in police protection, the designated officer.

(5) A recovery order shall name the child and—

   (a) any person who has parental responsibility for the child by virtue of a care order or emergency protection order; or

   (b) where the child is in police protection, the designated officer.

(6) Premises may only be specified under subsection (3)(d) if it appears to the court that there are reasonable grounds for believing the child to be on them.

(7) In this section—

   "an authorised person" means—

      (a) any person specified by the court;

      (b) any constable;

      (c) any person who is authorised—

         (i) after the recovery order is made; and

         (ii) by a person who has parental responsibility for the child by virtue of a care order or an emergency protection order,

         to exercise any power under a recovery order; and

PART V

"the designated officer" means the officer designated for the purposes of section 46.

(8) Where a person is authorised as mentioned in subsection (7)(c)—

(a) the authorisation shall identify the recovery order; and

(b) any person claiming to be so authorised shall, if asked to do so, produce some duly authenticated document showing that he is so authorised.

(9) A person shall be guilty of an offence if he intentionally obstructs an authorised person exercising the power under subsection (3)(b) to remove a child.

(10) A person guilty of an offence under this section shall be liable on summary conviction to a fine not exceeding level 3 on the standard scale.

(11) No person shall be excused from complying with any request made under subsection (3)(c) on the ground that complying with it might incriminate him or his spouse of an offence; but a statement or admission made in complying shall not be admissible in evidence against either of them in proceedings for an offence other than perjury.

(12) Where a child is made the subject of a recovery order whilst being looked after by a local authority, any reasonable expenses incurred by an authorised person in giving effect to the order shall be recoverable from the authority.

(13) A recovery order shall have effect in Scotland as if it had been made by the Court of Session and as if that court had had jurisdiction to make it.

(14) In this section "the court", in relation to Northern Ireland, means a magistrates' court within the meaning of the Magistrates' Courts (Northern Ireland) Order 1981.

S.I. 1981/1675 (N.I. 26).

Refuges for children at risk.

51.—(1) Where it is proposed to use a voluntary home or registered children's home to provide a refuge for children who appear to be at risk of harm, the Secretary of State may issue a certificate under this section with respect to that home.

(2) Where a local authority or voluntary organisation arrange for a foster parent to provide such a refuge, the Secretary of State may issue a certificate under this section with respect to that foster parent.

(3) In subsection (2) "foster parent" means a person who is, or who from time to time is, a local authority foster parent or a foster parent with whom children are placed by a voluntary organisation.

(4) The Secretary of State may by regulations—

(a) make provision as to the manner in which certificates may be issued;

(b) impose requirements which must be compiled with while any certificate is in force; and

(c) provide for the withdrawal of certificates in prescribed circumstances.

(5) Where a certificate is in force with respect to a home, none of the provisions mentioned in subsection (7) shall apply in relation to any person providing a refuge for any child in that home.

(6) Where a certificate is in force with respect to a foster parent, none of those provisions shall apply in relation to the provision by him of a refuge

for any child in accordance with arrangements made by the local authority or voluntary organisation.

(7) The provisions are—

(a) section 49;

(b) section 71 of the Social Work (Scotland) Act 1968 (harbouring children who have absconded from residential establishments etc.) so far as it applies in relation to anything done in England and Wales; 1968 c. 49.

(c) section 32(3) of the Children and Young Persons Act 1969 (compelling, persuading, inciting or assisting any person to be absent from detention, etc.), so far as it applies in relation to anything done in England and Wales; 1969 c. 54.

(d) section 2 of the Children Abduction Act 1984. 1984 c. 37.

52.—(1) Without prejudice to section 93 or any other power to make such rules, rules of court may be made with respect to the procedure to be followed in connection with proceedings under this Part. Rules and regulations.

(2) The rules may, in particular make provision—

(a) as to the form in which any application is to be made or direction is to be given;

(b) prescribing the persons who are to be notified of—

(i) the making, or extension, of an emergency protection order; or

(ii) the making of an application under section 45(4) or (8) or 46(7); and

(c) as to the content of any such notification and the manner in which, and person by whom, it is to be given.

(3) The Secretary of State may by regulations provide that, where—

(a) an emergency protection order has been made with respect to a child;

(b) the applicant for the order was not the local authority within whose area the child is ordinarily resident; and

(c) that local authority are of the opinion that it would be in the child's best interests for the applicant's responsibilities under the order to be transferred to them,

that authority shall (subject to their having complied with any requirements imposed by the regulations) be treated, for the purposes of this Act, as though they and not the original applicant had applied for, and been granted, the order.

(4) Regulations made under subsection (3) may, in particular, make provisions as to—

(a) the considerations to which the local authority shall have regard in forming an opinion as mentioned in subsection (3)(c); and

(b) the time at which responsibility under any emergency protection order is to be treated as having been transferred to a local authority.

Application for Emergency Protection Order

Section 44 The Children Act 1989

Date received by court

▶ Please use black ink. The notes on page 7 tell you what to do when you have completed the form.

▶ If there is more than one child you must fill in a separate form for each child.

▶ Please answer every part. If a part does not apply or you do not know what to say please say so. If there is not enough room continue on another sheet (put the child's name and the number of the part on the sheet).

▶ If you have any concerns about giving your address or that of the child or any other address requested in this form, you may give an alternative address where papers can be served. However, you must notify the court of the actual address on a separate form which you can get from the court office.

> Please speak to the court official immediately if you wish this application to be heard without giving Notice of the application to any other party.

━━━ THE ━━ CHILDREN ━━ ACT ━━━

Application to **The**   **[High] [County] [Magistrates'] Court**

for an Emergency Protection Order

Case No.

━━━ THE ━━ CHILDREN ━━ ACT ━━━

1 | About the child

(a) The name of the child is
Put the surname last

(b) The child is a   ☐ boy   ☐ girl

(c) The child was born on the
day	month	year		Age now

(d) The child usually lives at
See note on addresses at top of this form

(e) The child lives with
If the child does not live with a parent give the name of the person who is responsible for the child
☐ the child's mother   ☐ the child's father

(f) The child is also cared for by
Put the surname last

(g) The child is at present
☐ staying in a refuge
(Please give the address to the Court separately)
☐ not staying in a refuge

(h) If the child is temporarily living away from home, please say where he/she is living at present.
See note on addresses at the top of this form

(i) If child's identity is unknown state any details that identify the child
You may attach a recent photo of the child for the use of the court

(j) A Guardian ad litem
☐ has not been appointed
☐ has been appointed. The Guardian ad litem is

Name
Address
Tel.   Fax   Ref

(k) A solicitor
☐ has not been appointed to act for the child
☐ has been appointed to act for the child. The solicitor is

Name
Address
Tel.   Fax   Ref

━━━ THE ━━ CHILDREN ━━ ACT ━━━

CHA 34   1

2 | About the applicant

(a) The applicant's title is

☐ Mr ☐ Mrs ☐ Miss ☐ Ms Other *(say here)* [   ]

(b) The applicant's full name is
Put the surname last

[   ]

(c) The applicant is

☐ an officer of the [   ] local authority

☐ an officer of the National Society for the Prevention of Cruelty to Children

☐ a designated police officer

on behalf of [   ] local authority

☐ authorised by the Secretary of State

other *(say here)* [   ]

(d) The applicant's address is
State home or office

[   ]

(e) The applicant's telephone number and reference are

Tel.   *Ref*

(f) The applicant's solicitor is

Name

Address

Tel.   *Fax*   *Ref*

━━━━━━━━━━━━━━ THE ━━━━ CHILDREN ━━━ ACT ━━━━━━━━━━━━━━

3 | About the child's family

(a) The name of the child's mother is
Put the surname last

[   ]

(b) The mother usually lives at
See note on addresses at top of this form

[   ]

(c) The name of the child's father is
Put the surname last

[   ]

(d) The father usually lives at
See note on addresses at top of this form

[   ]

(e) The child's mother and father ☐ are living together   ☐ are living apart

2

3 | About the child's family (continued) –

(f) The father is

☐ married to the child's mother   ☐ married to someone else
☐ single   ☐ divorced

(g) The mother is

☐ married to the child's father   ☐ married to someone else
☐ single   ☐ divorced

(h) The child has

☐ no brothers and sisters under 18

Put the names, addresses and ages of all full brothers and sisters.

☐ brothers and sisters under 18. They are

If the child has halfbrothers or halfsisters, stepbrothers or stepsisters say who they are in (i) below.

If there are other children who are treated as children of the family say who they are in (i) below.

See note on addresses at the top of page 1

The name(s) of the brother(s) and sister(s)	Age (years)	The address(es) of the brother(s) and sister(s)

Do not include adoption orders

☐ No order has been made for any brother or sister

☐ No order for a brother or sister has been applied for

☐ An order has been made for a brother or sister

☐ An order for a brother or sister has been applied for

The name(s) of the child(ren)	The type of order	The court which made the order and when or which will hear the application Give the case number(s) where known	✓ if the order has been applied for	is in force

3

89

3 | About the child's family (continued) –

(i) There are other children ☐ under 18 who do not live with the family

☐ under 18 who live with the family.

They are

See note on addresses at the top of page 1.

The name of the child	The age of the child	Please give reasons why the child lives/does not live with the family	Address of children not living with the family

━━━━ THE ━━━ CHILDREN ━━━ ACT ━━━

4 | Parental responsibility

Some people have "parental responsibility" for a child.
The law says what "parental responsibility" is and which people have it.
These people include:

A the mother

B the father
if he was married to the child's mother
when the child was born

C the father
if he was not married to the child's mother
when the child was born
   but he now has a residence order

   or he now has a court order which gives him parental responsibility

   or he now has a formal "parental responsibility agreement" with the mother

   or he has since married the mother

D a guardian of the child

E someone who holds a custody or residence order

F a local authority which has a care order

G someone who holds an emergency protection order

H any man or woman who has adopted the child

The people who have parental responsibility for this child are believed to be

See note on addresses at the top of page 1.

Name	Address

━━━━ THE ━━━ CHILDREN ━━━ ACT ━━━

4

90

5 About other applications and orders which affect the child

(a) Other applications have ☐ not been made

☐ been made or will be made

What the application was for or will be for	When an application was made or will be made	The court which heard the application or which will hear the application. Give the case no. if known	The result

(b) Other orders ☐ have not been made
Please include orders that have been made but are no longer in force

☐ have been made. The orders are

Do not include adoption orders

The type of order	When was the order made	The court which made the order and the case number if known	√ if the order has expired (say when)	is in force

THE ■ CHILDREN ■ ACT

6 | About this application

(a) The grounds for making this application are

Delete one * if it does not apply.

1

☐ that there is reasonable cause to believe that the child is likely to suffer significant harm if

    * the child is not removed to accommodation provided by or on behalf of the applicant

    * the child does not remain in the place in which the child is currently being accommodated

Only an officer of a local authority should tick box 2

2

☐ that enquiries are being made with respect to the child's welfare under section 47(1)(b)

and

that those enquiries are being frustrated by access to the child being unreasonably refused to a person authorised to seek access and that there is reasonable cause to believe that access to the child is required as a matter of urgency

Only an authorised person under section 31 should tick box 3

3

☐ that there is reasonable cause to suspect that the child is suffering, or is likely to suffer, significant harm

and

enquiries are being made with respect to the child's welfare

and

those enquiries are being frustrated by access to the child being unreasonably refused to a person authorised to seek access and there is reasonable cause to believe that access to the child is required as a matter of urgency.

(b) These grounds exist because

(c) The applicant would like the court to order that

If you would like the Court to give directions on

- *contact*
- *a medical or psychiatric examination or other assessment of the child*
- *information on the whereabouts of the child*
- *authorisation for entry of premises*
- *authorisation to search for another child on the premises*

put these here.

6

92

6 About this application (continued) –

(d) This application will be heard   ☐   without notice being given to the other side

☐   with notice being given to the other side

(e) A report or relevant documentary evidence   ☐   is attached

☐   is not attached

(f) The respondents will be

- people with parental responsibility (see part 4)
- the child
- other people allowed by the Rules of Court.

  Please give details below

(i) Only give details of those respondents, whose names and addresses have not been given in part 4.

(ii) Please put the address where the respondent usually lives or where papers can be served. See note on addresses at the top of the form.

(iii) You will have to serve a copy of this application on each of the respondents.

The name of the respondent	The respondent's address

THE CHILDREN ACT

7 Declaration

I declare that the information I have given is correct and complete to the best of my knowledge

Signed

Date

THE CHILDREN ACT

What you (the person applying) must do next

▶ There is a Notice of Hearing on page 8. Fill in the boxes on the Notice.

▶ Take or send this form and any supporting documentation to the court with enough copies for each respondent to be served. The top copy will be kept by the court and the other copies given or sent back to you for service.

▶ Unless you are asking for this application to be heard without giving Notice to any other party, you must then serve the copies of the Application, the Notice of Hearing and any supporting documentation according to the Rules. You may also be required under the Rules to give notice of the proceedings to other people.

THE CHILDREN ACT

7

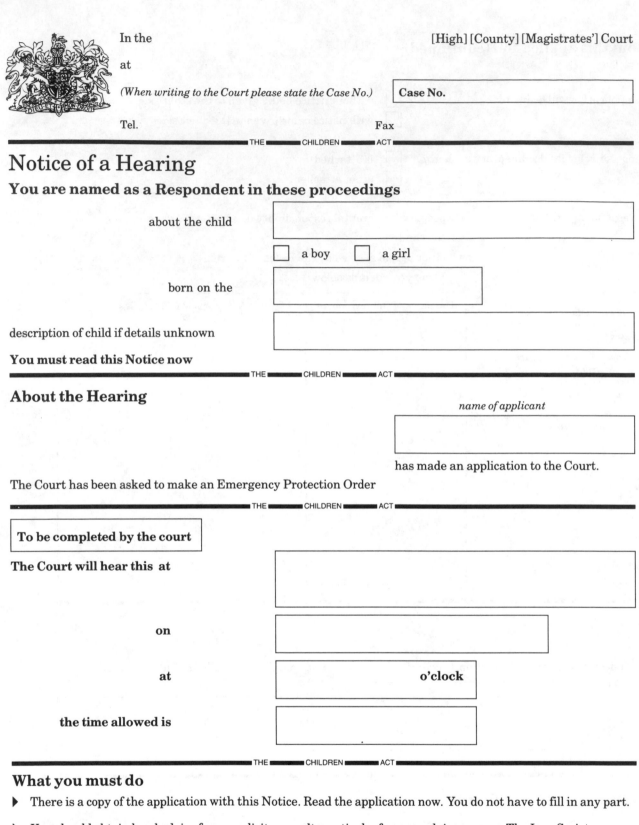

In the

at

(When writing to the Court please state the Case No.)

Tel.   Fax

[High] [County] [Magistrates'] Court

Case No.

━━━ THE ━━━ CHILDREN ━━━ ACT ━━━

Notice of a Hearing

You are named as a Respondent in these proceedings

about the child

☐ a boy   ☐ a girl

born on the

description of child if details unknown

You must read this Notice now

━━━ THE ━━━ CHILDREN ━━━ ACT ━━━

About the Hearing

name of applicant

has made an application to the Court.

The Court has been asked to make an Emergency Protection Order

━━━ THE ━━━ CHILDREN ━━━ ACT ━━━

To be completed by the court

The Court will hear this at

on

at   **o'clock**

the time allowed is

━━━ THE ━━━ CHILDREN ━━━ ACT ━━━

What you must do

▸ There is a copy of the application with this Notice. Read the application now. You do not have to fill in any part.

▸ You should obtain legal advice from a solicitor or, alternatively, from an advice agency. The Law Society administers a national panel of solicitors to represent children and other parties involved in proceedings relating to children. Addresses of solicitors (including panel members) and advice agencies can be obtained from the Yellow Pages and the Solicitors Regional Directory which can be found at Citizens Advice Bureaux, Law Centres and any local library.

▸ You may be entitled to legal aid. For certain Children Act proceedings, children, parents and those with parental responsibility will usually be eligible for legal aid automatically.

date

━━━ THE ━━━ CHILDREN ━━━ ACT ━━━

8

94

Application for a Child Assessment Order

Section 43 The Children Act 1989

Date received by court

▶ Please use black ink.
The notes on page 8 tell you what to do when you have completed the form.

▶ If there is more than one child you must fill in a separate form for each child.

▶ Please answer every part. If a part does not apply or you do not know what to say please say so. If there is not enough room continue on another sheet (put the child's name and the number of the part on the sheet).

▶ If you have any concerns about giving your address or that of the child or any other address requested in this form, you may give an alternative address where papers can be served. However, you must notify the court of the actual address on a separate form available from the court.

━━━ THE ━━ CHILDREN ━━ ACT ━━━

Application to **The**

for a Child Assessment Order

[High] [County] [Magistrates'] Court

Case No.

━━━ THE ━━ CHILDREN ━━ ACT ━━━

1 About the child

(a) The name of the child is
Put the surname last

(b) The child is a ☐ boy ☐ girl

(c) The child was born on the

day	month	year

Age now

(d) The child usually lives at
See note on addresses at top of this form

(e) The child lives with
If the child does not live with a parent please give the name of the person who is responsible for the child

☐ the child's mother ☐ the child's father

(f) The child is also cared for by
Put the surname last

(g) The child is at present

☐ staying in a refuge (Please give the address to the Court separately)

☐ not staying in a refuge

(h) If the child is temporarily living away from the usual address, please say where he/she is living at present
See note on addresses at top of this form

(i) A Guardian ad litem

☐ has not been appointed

☐ has been appointed. The Guardian ad litem is

Name
Address
Tel.   *Fax*   *Ref*

(j) A solicitor

☐ has not been appointed to act for the child

☐ has been appointed to act for the child. The solicitor is

Name
Address
Tel.   *Fax*   *Ref*

━━━ THE ━━ CHILDREN ━━ ACT ━━━

CHA 32

1

2 | About the applicant

(a) The applicant is

☐ **an officer of the** [_____] *local authority*

☐ an officer of the National Society for the Prevention of Cruelty to Children

☐ authorised by the Secretary of State to apply for this order.

(b) The applicant's full name is
Put the surname last

(c) The applicant's title is

☐ Mr   ☐ Mrs   ☐ Miss   ☐ Ms   Other *(say here)* [_____]

(d) The applicant's official address is

(e) The applicant's telephone number and reference are

Tel.   *Ref*

(f) The applicant's solicitor is

Name
Address

Tel.   *Fax*   *Ref*

(g) The social worker is

Name
Address

Tel.   *Fax.*   *Ref*

━━━━ THE ━━━━ CHILDREN ━━━━ ACT ━━━━

3 | About the child's family

(a) The full name of the child's mother is
Put the surname last

(b) The mother usually lives at
See note on addresses at the top of page 1

(c) The full name of the child's father is
Put the surname last

(d) The father usually lives at
See note on addresses at the top of page 1

(e) The child's mother and father

☐ are living together   ☐ are living apart

(f) The father is

☐ married to the child's mother   ☐ married to someone else
☐ single   ☐ divorced

(g) The mother is

☐ married to the child's father   ☐ married to someone else
☐ single   ☐ divorced

2

3 | **About the child's family (continued) –**

(h) The child has

☐ no brothers and sisters under 18

☐ brothers and sisters under 18. They are

See note on addresses at the top of page 1

Put the names, addresses and ages of all full brothers and sisters.

If the child has halfbrothers or halfsisters, stepbrothers or stepsisters say who they are in (i) below.

If there are other children who are treated as children of the family say who they are in (i) below.

The name(s) of the brother(s) and sister(s)	Age (years)	The address(es) of the brother(s) and sister(s)

(h) *(continued)*

☐ No order has been made for any brother or sister

☐ No order for a brother or sister has been applied for

☐ An order has been made for a brother or sister

Do not include adoption orders ☐ An order for a brother or sister has been applied for

The name(s) of the child(ren)	The type of order	The court which made the order and when or which will hear the application Include case number(s) where known	√ if the order has been applied for	is in force

(i) There are other children

☐ under 18 who do not live with the family

See note on addresses at the top of page 1 ☐ under 18 who live with the family.

They are

The name of the child	The age of the child	Please give reasons why the child lives/does not live with the family	Address of child not living with the family

THE ▬ CHILDREN ▬ ACT

3

4 | Parental responsibility

Some people have "parental responsibility" for a child.
The law says what "parental responsibility" is and which people have it.
These people include:

A the mother

B the father
if he was married to the child's mother *when* the child was born

C the father
if he was **not** married to the child's mother *when* the child was born
  but he now has a residence order
  or he now has a court order which gives him parental responsibility
  or he now has a formal "parental responsibility agreement" with the mother
  or he has since married the mother

D a guardian of the child

E someone who holds a custody or residence order

F a local authority which has a care order

G someone who holds an emergency protection order

H any man or woman who has adopted the child

The people who have parental responsibility for this child are believed to be

See note on addresses at the top of page 1

Name	Address

THE CHILDREN ACT

5 | About other applications and orders which affect the child

(a) Other applications have ☐ not been made

☐ been made or will be made

When an application was made or will be made	What the application was for or will be for	The court which heard the application or which will hear the application and the case number(s) if known	The result

THE CHILDREN ACT

5 About other applications and orders which affect the child (continued)

(b) Other orders
Do not include adoption orders

☐ have not been made

☐ have been made. The orders are

The type of order	When was the order made	The court which made the order and the case number if known	✓ if the order has expired (say when)	is in force

THE ■■■ CHILDREN ■■■ ACT ■

6 About this application

(a) The grounds for making this application are that

There is reasonable cause to suspect that the child is suffering, or is likely to suffer, significant harm

and

an assessment of the state of the child's health or development or of the way in which the child has been treated, is required to determine whether or not the child is suffering, or is likely to suffer, significant harm

and

it is unlikely that such an assessment will be made, or be satisfactory, in the absence of an order under this section.

(b) These grounds exist because

(Please give details of the type of assessment and other directions sought in parts 7 & 8)

THE ■■■ CHILDREN ■■■ ACT ■

5

99

6 | About this application (continued)

(c)   A report/relevant documentary evidence   ☐ is attached

☐ is not attached

(d)   The respondents will be

- people with parental responsibility
- the child
- other people allowed by the Rules of Court.

Please give details below

(i) You do not have to give the details of those respondents whose names and addresses have been given in part 4.

(ii) Please put the address where the respondent usually lives. See note on addresses at the top of page 1.

(iii) You will have to serve a copy of this application on the respondents.

The name of the respondent	The respondent's address

THE ▬▬ CHILDREN ▬▬ ACT ▬

7 | About the assessment

(a)   The type of assessment is

Please give a brief description of the type of assessment that will be made.

(b) The assessment will be carried out by

(c) The assessment will take place at

Tel.   *Fax*

(d) The assessment is expected to take [ ] days

(e) The child

☐ should not live away from home while being assessed

☐ should live away from home for all or part of the assessment because

(f) During any time the child will be away it is proposed that the arrangements for a contact with the child should be

The name of the person who may contact the child and the arrangements	The person's relationship to the child	Reason

8 | About other directions

The applicant would like further directions relating to the assess-ment. Include details as to whom the child should be produced.

9 | Declaration

I declare that the information I have given is correct and complete to the best of my knowledge

Signed

Date

What you (the person applying) must do next

▸ There is a Notice of Hearing on page 9. Fill in the boxes on the Notice.

▸ Take or send this form and any supporting documentation to the court with enough copies for each respondent to be served. The top copy will be kept by the court and the other copies given or sent back to you for service.

▸ You must then serve the copies of the Application, the Notice and any supporting documentation according to the Rules. You may also be required under the Rules to give notice of the proceedings to other people.

8

[High] [County] [Magistrates'] Court

Case No.

━━━━━ THE ━━━━━ CHILDREN ━━━━━ ACT ━━━━━

Notice of a [Hearing] [Directions Appointment]

You are named as a Respondent in these proceedings

about the child

☐ a boy   ☐ a girl

born on the

You must read this Notice now

━━━━━ THE ━━━━━ CHILDREN ━━━━━ ACT ━━━━━

About the [Hearing] [Directions Appointment]

name of applicant

has made an application to the Court.

The Court has been asked to make a Child Assessment Order

━━━━━ THE ━━━━━ CHILDREN ━━━━━ ACT ━━━━━

To be completed by the court

The Court will hear this at

on

at   **o'clock**

the time allowed is

━━━━━ THE ━━━━━ CHILDREN ━━━━━ ACT ━━━━━

What you must do

▶ There is a copy of the application with this Notice. Read the application now. You do not have to fill in any part.

▶ You should obtain legal advice from a solicitor or, alternatively, from an advice agency. The Law Society administers a national panel of solicitors to represent children and other parties involved in proceedings relating to children. Addresses of solicitors (including panel members) and advice agencies can be obtained from the Yellow Pages and the Solicitors Regional Directory which can be found at Citizens Advice Bureaux, Law Centres and any local library.

▶ You may be entitled to legal aid. For certain Children Act proceedings, children, parents and those with parental responsibility will usually be eligible for legal aid automatically.

date

━━━━━ THE ━━━━━ CHILDREN ━━━━━ ACT ━━━━━

103

ARMED SERVICES ARRANGEMENTS FOR CHILD PROTECTION

1. This Appendix offers guidance to cover Service families, for inclusion in local procedural handbooks.

General

2. The Service authorities seek to co-operate with statutory agencies and to support Service families where child abuse is suspected or occurs. The information they hold on any family can help in the assessment and review of child abuse cases.

Overseas

3. Procedures exist in all three Services overseas for the registration and monitoring of the protection of children, and the usual roles of confidentiality are observed.

3.1 When it appears that a child is in urgent need of care or control an officer having jurisdiction in relation to the child may order the child to be removed to and detained in a place of safety. If the officer makes an order to transfer the child to the United Kingdom so that care of the child can become the responsibility of the relevant local authority all necessary action will be arranged and agreed beforehand between the responsible agencies concerned.

3.2 New arrangements for dealing with the emergency protection of children of Service families abroad are introduced in the Armed Forces Act 1991. These provide for the officer having jurisdiction in relation to a child to make an order to remove the child or keep it in accommodation provided by or on behalf of the person who applied for the order. The grounds for making an order mirror those for emergency protection orders under the Children Act 1989.

3.3 Until these arrangements are brought into effect, probably in the middle of 1992, officers having jurisdiction retain their existing powers to make orders for removing children in need of urgent care and control to a place of safety.

3.4 Where a child of a Service family overseas is the subject of a place of safety order or the new protection order is returned to the United Kingdom he or she becomes the responsibility of the local authority. All necessary action will be arranged and agreed beforehand between the responsible agencies concerned.

United Kingdom

4. Service authorities through their internal instructions are made aware that the primary responsibility for the protection of children is the local authority's and that assistance should be given to enable them to fulfill their statutory obligations.

Army

5. The provisions of welfare support to any Army family whose children are considered to be at risk by a social services department is the responsibility of the Army Families Housing and Welfare Service (FHWS) and a small number of SSAFA qualified social workers are employed to assist. Social services departments should liaise with one of the 55 FHWS Commandants (Managers) who, together with their welfare staff, provide cover throughout the UK. Contact telephone numbers are given at the end of this Appendix.

6. The Naval Personal and Family Service (NPFS) provides qualified social work teams in three UK areas, each headed by an area officer. Their telephone numbers are given at the end of this Appendix.

Royal Air Force

7. Welfare support for families in the Royal Air Force is managed as a normal function of command and co-ordinated by each station's personnel officer; the Officer Commanding Personnel Management Squadron (OCPMS) or Officer Commanding Administrative Squadron (OC Admin Sqn), depending on the size of the station, and a small number of SSAFA qualified social workers are employed to assist. Whenever a child abuse investigation concerns the child of a serving member of the RAF, the social services department should notify the parents' unit, or if this is not known by contacting the OCPMS/OC Admin Sqn of the nearest RAF unit. Every RAF unit has an officer appointed to this duty and he will be familiar with child abuse procedures.

Movement of Service Families between UK and Overseas

8. The Soldiers' Sailors' and Airman's Families Association provides, at the request of the Ministry of Defence, a qualified social work and health visiting service for families of all Services on overseas stations.

8.1 Where there is a child protection plan in this country for a child in a Service family who are to move overseas, the social services department concerned should notify SSAFA in writing with full documentation, case conference notes, etc. to:

Assistant Director SSAFA UK
SSAFA
HQ UKLF
Old Sarum
Salisbury
Wiltshire SP4 6BN

This information is forwarded to the relevant SSAFA social worker overseas in order that:

(a) the case may be entered on the overseas British Forces Child Protection Register;

(b) the practitioners at the overseas base can be alerted, preferably before the planned departure; and

(c) appropriate support and supervision are provided to the family.

8.2 Similarly, when a Service family with a child in need of protection returns to the UK, it is SSAFA's responsibility to contact the social services department in whose area they will be living and ensure that full documentation is provided to assist in the management of the case.

9. Where there is a statutory involvement (e.g. supervision order) on a family moving overseas SSAFA will provide the necessary supervision and support as well as regular written reports to the local authority concerned.

10. UK Armed Service Contact Points

10.1 *Army*

Controller FHWS, HQ UKLF Salisbury 0722 336222 Old Sarum Mil. ext 8221/8226

Principal Commandants FHWS

North East   York 0904 659811 ext 2541

North West	Preston 0772 260473 ext 2473
West	Shrewsbury 0743 236060 ext 2431
East	Colchester 0206 575121 ext 2064
South East	Aldershot 0252 24431 ext 2166
South West	Bulford Camp 0980 33371 ext 2865
London	071 930 4466 ext 2264
Scotland	Edinburgh 031 336 1761 ext 2107
Wales	Brecon 0874 3111 ext 2305
Lypiatt Families Centre	Corsham, Wilts 02258 10358 ext 4525

10.2 *Royal Navy*

Western Area	Plymouth 0752 568611
Eastern Area	Portsmouth 0705 820932/826774
Northern Area	Rosyth 0383 416747/410111

10.3 *Royal Air Force*

See paragraph 5

10.4 *Northern Ireland*

Army

Principal Commandant FHWS   Lisburn 08462 665111 ext 42734

Royal Navy   NI interests covered by Northern Area

Royal Air Force   Officer Commanding
Administrative Squadron
RAF Aldergrove
BFPO 808
08494 22051 ext 31302/31338

SSAFA   Lisburn 08462 609361 ext 42008

10.5 *SSAFA*

Director of Social Work 071 403 8783
Assistant Director of Social Work 0722 336222 ext 8245/8257

USAF

11. Each local authority with an American base in their area should have established liaison arrangements with the base commander and relevant staff. British child protection and care legislation should be set out and requirements made clear to the USAF authorities so that local authorities can ensure that they are able to fulfill their statutory duties.

CHILD PROTECTION REGISTER

This Appendix lists the data to be held on the child protection register.

Part I: Identification

1. Child's full name, other names known to be used, home address, sex, date and place of birth.

2. Location (if not at home).

3. Legal status of child when first placed on the register (register to be amended on every change in legal status).

4. Full names (including maiden names), known other names used and addresses of parents or others caring for the child and the name and address of any other adult members of, or regular visitors to the household, together with information on their relationship to the child.

5. Details of any relevant offences of any person mentioned at 4 above.

6. Full names, dates of birth and sex of other children in the household, care status where appropriate and whether they are also on the child protection register.

Part II: Nature of Abuse

7. Date of first referral to statutory agency, and source of referral.

8. Indication of categories of abuse in the case. (Use categories as set out in Department of Health statistical return CPR1. See Part 6.)

Part III: Key Worker and Core Group

9. Name of key worker and telephone number.

10. Other agencies providing services to the child and family, including identification of core group.

11. GP's name, address and telephone number.

12. HV's name, address and telephone number.

13. Child's school, play group, nursery or childminder, if any; including name of designated teacher, etc. and telephone number.

Part IV: Child Protection Plan

14. Date of plan (i.e. registration date).

15. Date when parents or carers told of registration and initial plan.

16. Programme of review (i.e. timing, method, etc.).

17. Date of reviews.

18. Date when inter-agency review ended (i.e. de-registration) or date when child moved from area, new address and arrangements made for handover to agencies in new area e.g. conferences held, records transferred, etc.

19. Record of all enquiries to the register.

All staff involved with the child and family should notify changes in this information to the key worker so that the register may be kept up to date.

AREA CHILD PROTECTION COMMITTEES (ACPCs)

1. The ACPC must concern itself with the full range of services provided by the agencies described in Part 4 of this Guide. It is recommended that formal membership should include senior managers or professionals representing the following main services (although the exact composition is a matter to be agreed locally):

(a) **Social Service Agencies**

    i.   local authority social services department

    ii.   National Society for the Prevention of Cruelty to Children (NSPCC) where they are active in the local authority area

(b) **Health Authority**

    i.   Management of District Health Authority(ies) in the local authority area

    ii.   Medical and psychiatric services professional representative(s)

    iii.   Nursing representative(s)

(c) **Family Health Services Authority**

    i.   Management of FHSAs in the local authority area

    ii.   General practitioner representative(s) of the local medical committee(s) in the local authority area

(d) **Education Service**

    i.   Local authority education department

    ii.   Teacher representative (normally a head teacher)

(e) **Police**

(f) **Probation Service**

(g) **Armed Services** – where appropriate and particularly if there is a major service base in the area.

2. In addition, it will be important for the Committee to establish links with:

    i.   Local authority housing departments;

    ii.   General Dental Practitioner Services;

    iii.   Local Social Security offices;

    iv.   Education establishments not maintained by the local authority;

    v.   Voluntary agencies providing relevant services;

    vi.   Organisations representing religious and cultural interests.

CONTENT AND FORMAT OF LOCAL PROCEDURAL HANDBOOKS

1. The structure and content of local procedural handbooks concerned with the handling of inter-agency issues should be standardised. The recommended standard content is:

Section I: Law and Definitions

(a) The legal framework for work to protect children from harm
(b) The criteria for placing a child's name on the child protection register
(c) The categories of abuse under which a child can be registered;

Section II: Who is Involved

(a) The roles of statutory agencies and how child protection work fits into the rest of their work and the child welfare responsibilities of authorities – particularly to children being looked after by a local authority
(b) The contribution of other agencies and independent practitioners;

Section III: Referral and Recognition

(a) How members of the public and staff locally should refer any concern they have about individual children
(b) The central role of local authority social services department (or the NSPCC) and the police in investigating suspected cases
(c) The steps that the social services department (or the NSPCC) and the police will take to investigate cases, including holding strategy discussions or meetings
(d) The contributions of other agencies, including the role of medical and health staff in seeking to establish the significance of injuries or other evidence of possible abuse;

Section IV: Immediate Protection and Planning the Investigation

(a) How staff in other agencies may be involved in inter-agency discussions aimed at developing an agreed plan of action
(b) To describe the role of the key worker who will have case responsibility
(c) How parents should be involved in the investigation;

Section V: Investigation and Initial Assessment

See Para 5 paragraph 5.14;

Section VI: Child Protection Conference and Decision Making about the Need for Registration

See Part 5 paragraph 5.15 and Part 6;

Section VII: Comprehensive Child Protection Assessment and Planning

See Part 5 paragraph 5.16;

Section VIII: Implementation, Review and De-registration

See Part 5 paragraph 5.18 and Part 6;

Section IX: Other

Advice on special circumstances, for example: children of Service families (see Appendix 3); organised abuse; abuse by professionals or cases where it is known or suspected that a child may be about to be subjected to female genital mutilation;

Section X: Local Agency Procedures

Agreed procedures to be followed by individual agencies for their own staff.

FORMAT

2. The recommended format of handbooks is:

(a) A loose-leaf form, to aid regular review and revision of the material;

(b) Full indexes should be provided, with a summary page showing important telephone contacts and addresses;

(c) Concisely worded, short paragraphs;

(d) Good typography to highlight important points.

CHILD ABUSE MANAGEMENT INFORMATION

The recommended information that should be provided to the ACPC quarterly is:

I. Information from the child protection register

(a) Current cases: information on the characteristics of the children currently on the register, e.g. age/sex, type of abuse, length of time on register, etc.

(b) Sources of original referrals for investigation of cases currently on the register, including information on number of referals from each source.

(c) Information on any cases which have been placed on the child protection register for which there is no allocated key worker.

(d) Cases removed from the register:

The number and types of cases for which formalised inter-agency collaboration has ceased, i.e. cases taken off the register or cases transferred to another area.

II. Information from the record on enquiries to the register

(a) Number and source (i.e. agency) of enquiries about children on the register.

(b) Number and source (i.e. agency) of enquiries about children not on the register.

III. Information related to the use of statutory powers on an emergency basis

(a) Number of applications for emergency protection orders with reason for the application.

(b) Number granted.

(c) Eventual child care status.

IV. Information from other records

The level of child abuse work e.g. number, attendance (numbers and details of who represented, including parental and child attendance), frequency and average duration of case conferences held.

V. Reports from constituency members of the ACPC

Information on any major internal or external factors affecting the level of service provision in child protection work. Details of any initiatives in prevention of child abuse.

The ACPC annual report should be produced by the end of June each year and contain information relating to the financial year (April to March). The recommended format is:

Section I: Prevention

This should include a description of the action taken to identify vulnerable children and families and provide help and support.

This should include details of:

- contributions from constituent agencies, including new developments and identification of problems in maintaining services;
- preventive schemes, including evaluation and the views of users;
- collaborative schemes between statutory and voluntary groups;
- publicity to alert and educate the public to child protection issues;

Section II: Protection

This should include:

- a description of action taken to ensure that members of the public and practitioners in all agencies are aware how they can report any concern they have for individual children;
- information on the number of individual cases investigated, the plans of action and number of cases concluded;
- information on trends over time, different types of abuse, etc.;
- information on any cases which are not allocated to a key worker;
- a description of the outcome of any case review or inquiry into serious cases of abuse.

Information (in anonymous terms) to compile this element of the report would be drawn from the regular management information provided to the ACPC (see Appendix 7). *This section should include a statement of objectives for the past year, details of any inter-agency quality control systems and summaries of the work of any sub-committees.*

Section III: Policy and Procedures

This should include a description of relevant agency or inter-agency policy and procedural changes related to child abuse made during the year and to set out forward plans for the year ahead, *including a statement of objectives.*

Section IV: Training

This should include a description of action taken by individual agencies and collectively to:

- reinforce the awareness of staff over the indicators of child abuse;
- improve knowledge and skills of practitioners in handling of child abuse cases;
- identify requirements for training on an inter-agency basis and develop plans for meeting those needs.

This section should include details of the ACPC training strategy, the results of training evaluation exercises, the number and types of professionals trained and details of funding arrangements.

GLOSSARY OF TERMS USED IN WORKING TOGETHER

(with acknowledgement to the Open University)

This Glossary is intended to provide relatively simple explanations of the most important terms and phrases used in the text. There are basically three kinds of entry. First, we have included phrases given a specific meaning within the Children Act 1989 (such as 'accommodation'). These are intended to be generally useful to aid familiarisation with the new terminology. Where appropriate we have added cross-references to the Act itself; where we quote directly from the Act we use quotation marks. We have included terms which have specified meanings in child care work (such as 'assessment'), to clarify what these mean in the context in which we have used them. We have tried to be as comprehensive as practicable, without overburdening the text.

Accommodation

Being provided with accommodation replaces the old voluntary care concept. It refers to a service that the local authority provides to the parents of children in need, and their children. The child is not in care when s/he is being provided with accommodation; nevertheless the local authority has a number of duties towards children for whom it is providing accommodation, including the duty to discover the child's wishes regarding the provision of accommodation and to give them proper consideration [S20].

Agency

This term covers both public bodies and voluntary organisations.

Area Child Protection Committee (ACPC)

Based upon the boundaries of the local authority, it provides a forum for developing, monitoring and reviewing the local child protection policies, and promoting effective and harmonious co-operation between the various agencies involved. Although there is some variation from area to area, each committee is made up of representatives of the key agencies, who have authority to speak and act on their agency's behalf. ACPCs issue guidelines about procedures, tackle significant issues that arise, offer advice about the conduct of cases in general, make policy and review progress on prevention, and oversee inter-agency training.

Assessment

In the context of "Working Together", this term is used in several different ways. Definitions are as follows:

Initial assessment
An agreed multi-disciplinary composite report on the child's current health and welfare in the context of his/her family which will enable participants at a case conference to plan the child's immediate future.

Medical assessment
A specific examination by a doctor for a definite purpose e.g. a court request or as part of a child's health surveillance programme. The medical assessment may be more wide-ranging than a physical examination of the child and may in addition include comment on development and behaviour. The medical assessment may include recommendations for the ongoing care of the child within a medical context.

Developmental assessment

An objective assessment of a child, often to some agreed protocol, carried out by a doctor, health visitor or child psychologist, for the purpose of determining the child's developmental level. Such assessments carried out in a serial way would provide information on a child's developmental progress. Developmental assessments are normally part of the DHA child health surveillance programme, but may be carried out at other times.

Special educational needs assessment

A compilation of reports from various professionals to assist the local education authority to place the child in an educational setting compatible with his abilities. This assessment is carried out under the Education Act 1981.

Health assessment

An examination undertaken by the health visitor or school nurse to ascertain the child's health status. The health assessment will include information on height and weight, immunisation status, and vision and hearing.

Comprehensive assessment

A structured time limited exercise to collect and evaluate information about the child and his family on which to base long term decisions. (See 'Protecting Children: A guide for social workers undertaking comprehensive assessment'.)

Family assessment

A report prepared over a period of time to assess the functioning of a particular family in relation to the needs of a child. The assessment is usually undertaken by a social worker but may be undertaken by a psychologist or family centre worker.

Authority

A public body which has statutory powers or duties or both.

Authorised person

In relation to care and supervision proceedings, a person other than the local authority, authorised by the Secretary of State to bring proceedings under S31 of the Act. This covers the NSPCC and its officers.

Care order

An order made by the court under S31(1)(a) of the Act placing the child in the care of the designated local authority. A care order includes an interim care order except where express provision to the contrary is made [S31(11)] (see Appendix 2).

Child protection

Child protection conference

In a child care context, a formal meeting attended by representatives from all the agencies concerned with the child's welfare (increasingly this includes the child's parents, and the Act promotes this practice). Its purpose is to gather together and evaluate all the relevant information about a child, and plan any immediate action which may be necessary to protect the child (e.g. seeking a court order). Where the meeting decides that the child and family need support, a keyworker will be appointed to co-ordinate an inter-agency plan for work with the child and the family, and the child's name (plus those of any other children living in the same household) may be entered on the child protection register (see Part 6).

Child assessment order

An order under S43 of the Act. The order requires any person who can do so to produce the child for an assessment and comply with the terms of the order (see Appendix 2).

Child protection register

A central record of all children in a given area for whom support is being provided via inter-agency planning. Generally, these are children considered to be at risk of abuse or neglect. The register is usually maintained and run by social services departments under the responsibility of a custodian (an experienced social worker able to provide advice to any professional making enquiries about the child) (see Part 6).

Children in need

A child is "in need" if:

"(a) he is unlikely to achieve or maintain, or have the opportunity of achieving or maintaining, a reasonable standard of health or development without the provision for him of services by a local authority under this Part (Part III of the Children Act 1989);

(b) his health or development is likely to be significantly impaired, or further impaired, without the provision for him of such services; or

(c) he is disabled" [S17(10)].

Children living away from home

Children who are not being looked after by the local authority but are nevertheless living away from home, e.g. children in independent schools. The local authority has a number of duties towards such children e.g. to take reasonably practicable steps to ensure that their welfare is being adequately safeguarded and promoted.

Complaints procedure

The procedure that the local authority must set up to hear representations regarding the provision of services under Part III of the Act from a number of persons, including the child, the parents and "such other person as the authority consider has a sufficient interest in the child's welfare to warrant his representations being considered by them" [S26(3)]. This procedure must contain an independent element.

Contact

Between a child and another person includes visits, stays, outings and communication by letter and telephone. Under S34 of the Act the local authority is under a duty to allow a child in care reasonable contact with a number of persons, including the child's parents.

Contact Order

An order "requiring the person with whom a child lives, or is to live, to allow the child to visit or stay with the person named in the order, or for that person and the child otherwise to have contact with each other" [S8].

Court welfare officer

An officer appointed to provide a report for the court about the child and the child's family situation and background. The court welfare officer will usually be a probation officer. The court may request either the local authority or the court welfare officer to prepare a report [S7(1)].

A person provides day care if s/he looks after one or more children under the age of 8 on non-domestic premises for more than 2 hours in any day [S71]. In relation to the local authority provision of day care, it refers to any form of supervised activity provided for children during the day [S18(4)].

The role of the designated senior doctor

Commissioning authorities (District Health Authorities or General Practice fundholders) should ensure that all provider units concerned with children (directly managed units or NHS Trusts) have sound child protection policies and procedures in place. In drawing up contracts with provider units commissioning authorities are advised to enlist the services of a senior doctor experienced in child protection to advise on the content of contracts in relation to the protection of children. The commissioning authority will want to ensure that in all provider units concerned with the care of children:

i)   child protection policies are in agreement with ACPC policy;

ii) effective communication systems exist to coordinate work between different provider units (hospital, community child health service, school health service) including an efficient system for transferring records;

iii) a source of information and advice on child protection is available to all doctors and other health professionals who come into contact with children;

iv) doctors know how, and under what circumstances, to contact social services departments about use of the child protection register.

Each provider unit concerned with children should have, or be able to call on the services of, at least one senior doctor with a high level of skill and expertise in child protection to:

i)   identify the training needs of medical staff working with children in relation to child protection, including child protection procedures, and arrange for these needs to be met. Wherever possible training should be multidisciplinary,

ii) ensure the provision of a source of information and advice on child protection, including clinical aspects and procedures, either personally or through well defined delegation arrangements to named posts,

iii) act as a reference point for other agencies (i.e. Social Services Departments, Local Education Authorities, Family Health Service Authorities, NSPCC, voluntary organisations) so that advice is coordinated for these bodies.

Designated staff in the education service

In every school there should be a senior member of staff with specific responsibility for co-ordinating action within the school and for liaising with social services departments and other agencies over suspected or actual cases of child abuse. The designated teacher's role is to ensure that locally established procedures are followed, and particularly to act as the channel for communicating to the social services department relevant concerns expressed by any member of the school staff about individual children. Investigation of cases must be left to the social services department or other appropriate agencies.

A senior officer of the youth service should have a similar role to that of designated teachers.

In every local education authority there should be a senior officer with LEA-wide responsibility for co-ordinating education service – including youth service – policy and action on child protection. This designated officer should ensure that the locally established procedures, including the arrangements for designated teachers, are in place; should be the authority level point of contact with the social services department and other agencies; and should normally be the LEA's representative on the ACPC.

Designated senior nurse and midwife

The Health Authority should designate a senior nurse and a senior midwife whose duties should include;

– ensuring that effective child protection policies are in place in all provider units, Directly Managed Units (DMUs) and NHS Trusts and they are in agreement with ACPC policy;

– setting up an effective communication system to co-ordinate work between provider units, DMUs and NHS Trusts;

– acting as a reference point for other agencies SSD, LEA, FHSA, Police, NSPCC etc;

– monitoring the system for transferring nursing and midwifery records within and between health authorities;

– ensuring that provider units are aware of the names of the children in their care who are on the child protection register;

– identifying training needs.

Day to day monitoring and provision of training lies with professional managers.

Duty to investigate

The local authority is under a duty to investigate in a number of situations. The general investigative duty arises where the local authority has "reasonable cause to suspect that a child who lives, or is found, in their area is suffering, or is likely to suffer, significant harm", it must make such enquiries as it considers necessary to enable it to decide whether it should take any action to safeguard or promote the child's welfare [S47(1)].

Emergency protection order

An order under S44 which the court can make if it is satisfied that a child is likely to suffer significant harm, or where enquiries are being made with respect to the child and they are being frustrated by the unreasonable refusal of access to the child. The order gives the applicant parental responsibility for the child [S44] (see Appendix 2).

Family assistance order

An order under S16 of the Act requiring either a probation officer or a social worker to "advise, assist and befriend" a named person for a period of 6 months or less. The named person can be the child's parents, guardian, those with whom the child lived or who had contact with the child, and the child him/herself.

Family centre

A centre which the child and parents, and any other person looking after the child, can attend for occupational and recreational activities, advice, guidance or counselling, and accommodation while receiving such advice, guidance or counselling [Sched 2, para 9].

Family proceedings

These are defined in S8(3) as any proceedings under the inherent jurisdiction of the High Court in relation to children; and under Parts 1, II and IV of the Act, the Matrimonial Causes Act 1973, the Domestic Violence and Matrimonial Proceedings Act 1976, the Adoption Act 1976, the Domestic Proceeding and Magistrates' Courts Act 1978, ss1 and 9 of the Matrimonial Homes Act 1983, and Part III of the Matrimonial and Family Proceedings Act 1984. Note: proceedings under Part V of the Children Act 1989, i.e. orders for the protection of children, are not family proceedings.

Family proceedings court

The new court at the level of the Magistrates' Court to hear proceedings under the Children Act 1989. The magistrates will be selected from a new panel, known as the Family Panel, and will be specially trained.

Guardian ad litem (GAL)

A person appointed by the court to investigate a child's circumstances and to report to the court (S41). The GAL can appoint a solicitor for the child. In some cases the Official Solicitor acts as the GAL.

Guidance

Local authorities are required to act in accordance with the guidance issued by the Secretary of State. However, guidance does not have the full force of law but is intended as a series of statements of good practice and may be quoted or used in court proceedings.

Injunction

An order made by the court prohibiting an act or requiring its cessation. Under the Domestic Violence and Matrimonial Proceedings Act 1976 the County Court has the power to make injunctions. Injunctions can be either interlocutory (i.e. temporary, pending the outcome of the full hearing) or perpetual.

Inter-agency plan

A plan devised jointly by the agencies concerned in a child's welfare which co-ordinates the services they provide. Its aim is to ensure that the support offered meets all the child's needs, so far as this is practicable, and that duplication and rivalry are avoided. The plan should specify goals to be achieved, resources and services to be provided, the allocation of responsibilities, and arrangements for monitoring and review.

Interim care order

An order made by the court under S38 placing the child in the care of the designated local authority. There are provisions as to its duration, with an initial period of 8 weeks.

Interim supervision order, see Interim care order

Investigative interview

The preferred term for an interview conducted with a child as part of an assessment following concerns that the child may have been abused (most notably cases of suspected sexual abuse).

Judicial review

An order from the Divisional Court quashing a local authority decision, a declaration in a particular case as to what the law is, or an order directing the authority to take or not to take particular steps. The Divisional Court usually does not substitute its own decision but sends the matter back to the authority for reconsideration.

Keyworker

A social worker allocated specific responsibility for a particular child.

Looked after

A child is looked after when s/he is in local authority care or is being provided with accommodation by the local authority [S22(1)].

Monitoring

Where plans for a child, and the child's safety and well-being, are systematically appraised on a routine basis. Its function is to oversee the child's continued welfare and enable any necessary action or change to be instigated speedily, and at a managerial level, to ensure that proper professional standards are being maintained.

Official Solicitor

An officer of the Supreme Court who acts on behalf of children in certain cases. When representing a child the Official Solicitor may act both as a solicitor and as a guardian ad litem.

Paramountcy principle

The principle that the welfare of the child is the paramount consideration in proceedings concerning children.

Parental responsibility

Defined as "all the rights, duties, powers, responsibilities and authority which by law a parent of a child has in relation to the child and his property" [S3(1)]. Parental responsibility can be exercised by persons who are not the child's biological parent and can be shared among a number of persons. It can be acquired by agreement or court order.

Parties

Parties to proceedings are entitled to attend the hearing, present their case and examine witnesses. The Act envisages that children will automatically be parties in care proceedings. Anyone with parental responsibility for the child will also be a party to such proceedings, as will the local authority. Others may be able to acquire party status. A person with party status will be eligible for legal aid in order to be legally represented at the hearing. If you have party status you are also able to appeal against the decision. Others who are not parties may be entitled to make representations. For further information on this, refer to the Rules of Court.

Permanency planning

Deciding on the long-term future of children who have been moved from their families. Its purpose is to ensure them a permanent, stable and secure upbringing, either within their original family or by providing high-quality alternative parenting (for example, living permanently with grandparents or other relatives, or being adopted). Its aim is to avoid long periods of insecurity or repeated disruptions in children's lives.

Police protection

S46 allows the police to detain a child or prevent his/her removal for up to 72 hours if they believe that the child would otherwise suffer significant harm. There are clear duties on the police to consult the child, if this is practicable, and to notify various persons of their action, e.g. the child's parents and the local authority.

Preliminary hearing

A hearing to clarify matters in dispute, to agree evidence, and to give directions as to the timetable of the case and the disclosure of evidence.

Prohibited steps order

An order that "no step which could be taken by a parent in meeting his parental responsibility for a child, and which is of a kind specified in the order, shall be taken by any person without the consent of the court" [S8(1)].

Recovery order

An order which the court can make when there is reason to believe that a child who is in care, the subject of an emergency protection order or in police protection has been unlawfully taken or kept away from the responsible person, or has run away or is staying away from the responsible person, or is missing. The effect of the recovery order is to require any person who is in a position to do so to produce the child on request, to authorise the removal of the child by any authorised person, and to require any person who has information as to the child's whereabouts to disclose that information, if asked to do so, to a constable or officer of the court [S50].

Refuge

S51 enables "safe houses" legally to provide care for children who have run away from home or local authority care. However, a recovery order can be obtained in relation to a child who has run away to a refuge.

Regulations

Refer to the supplementary powers and duties issued by the Secretary of State under the authority of the Act. These cover a wide range of issues, from secure accommodation to the procedure for considering representations (including complaints), and have the full force of law.

Rehabilitation

In a child care context, the process of working with children and parents, and providing resources and support to enable children to return home to be brought up in their families, for the children's needs to be met, and to help overcome the problems that led to their needing to live away.

Representations

See Complaints procedure.

Residence order

An order "settling the arrangements to be made as to the person with whom a child is to live" [S8(1)].

Responsible person

In relation to a supervised child, "any person who has parental responsibility for the child, any any other person with whom the child is living". With their consent the responsible person can be required to comply with certain obligations [Sched 3, paras 1 and 3].

Review

Under S26 local authorities are under a duty to conduct regular reviews in order to monitor the progress of children they are looking after. When holding reviews local authorities must comply with their duties as given in S22. Reviews are opportunities to consider progress and any problems and changes in circumstances, and to resolve difficulties, set new goals and plan for the future. They are usually attended by all those with significant responsibilities for the child. The child and his/her parents should also attend, and be given help and support to participate in the decision making and to make sure their views and wishes are known [S26].

In addition to the statutory review, there are other reviews which are covered in "Working Together".

Child protection review
A review of the inter-agency child protection plan by a meeting or receipt of written reports.

Agency case review
A review of an individual case by one of the agencies of the Area Child Protection Committee (ACPC).

ACPC case review
This is a composite report based on an overview of the reports supplied by individual agencies which make up the ACPC.

Rules

Rules of Court made by the Lord Chancellor lay down the procedural rules which govern the operation of the courts under the Children Act 1989.

Section 8 orders

The four new orders contained in the Act which, to varying degrees, regulate the exercise of parental responsibility.

Significant harm

S31(10) states: "Where the question of whether harm suffered by a child is significant turns on the child's health or development, his health or development shall be compared with that which could reasonably be expected of a similar child".

Specific issue order

"giving directions for the purpose of determining a specific question which has arisen, or which may arise, in connection with any aspect of parental responsibility for a child" [S8(1)].

Supervision order

An order under S31(1)(b) and including, except where express contrary provision is made, an interim supervision order under S38.

Timetables

Under the Act the court, pursuant to the principle of avoiding delay because it is harmful for the child, has the power to draw up a timetable and give directions for the conduct of the case in any proceedings in which the making of a Section 8 order arises, and in applications for care and supervision orders [SS11 and 32].

Ward of court

A child who, as the subject of wardship proceedings, is under the protection of the High Court. No important decision can be taken regarding the child while s/he is a ward of court without the consent of the Wardship Court.

Welfare report

S7 of the Act gives the court the power to request a report on any question in respect of a child under the Act. The report can be presented by either a probation officer or an officer of the local authority. Section 7(4) provides that regardless of any rule of law to the contrary, the court may take account of any statement contained in the report and any evidence given in respect of matters referred to in the report as long as the court considers them relevant.

Written agreement

The agreement arrived at between the local authority and the parents of children for whom it is providing services. These agreements are part of the partnership model that is seen as good practice under the Act.

Printed in the United Kingdom for HMSO
Dd   295014   c1730   10/91   6157